United States
Department
of Agriculture

Forest Service

**Rocky Mountain
Research Station**

Resource Bulletin
RMRS-RB-13

June 2012

The Four Corners Timber Harvest and Forest Products Industry, 2007

I0435053

Steven W. Hayes, Todd A. Morgan, Erik C. Berg, Jean M. Daniels and Mike T. Thompson

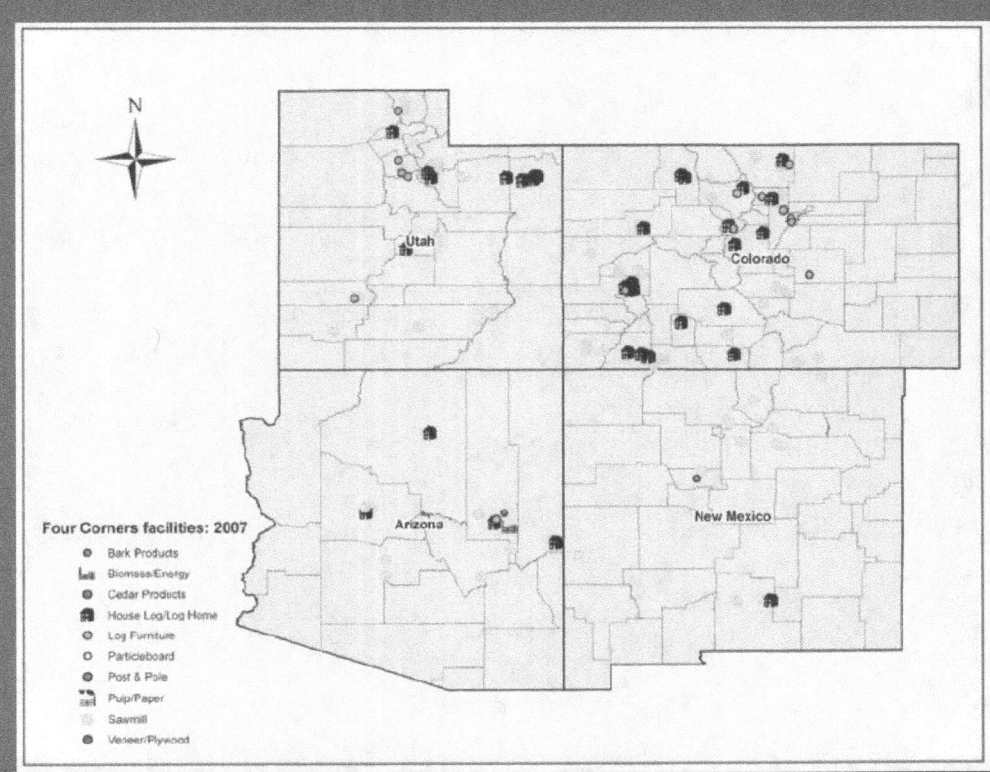

Abstract

This report traces the flow of timber harvested in the "Four Corners" States (Arizona, Colorado, New Mexico, and Utah) during calendar year 2007, describes the composition and operations of the region's primary forest products industry, and quantifies volumes and uses of wood fiber. Historical wood products industry changes are discussed, as well as trends in timber harvest, production, and sales of primary wood products.

Keywords: forest economics, lumber production, mill residue, primary forest products, timber products

Authors

Steven W. Hayes is a Research Forester, **Todd A. Morgan** is Director of Forest Industry Research, and **Erik C. Berg** is a Research Forester, Bureau of Business and Economic Research, The University of Montana, Missoula, Montana.

Jean M. Daniels is a Research Forester, U.S. Department of Agriculture, Forest Service, Pacific Northwest Research Station, Forestry Sciences Laboratory, Portland, Oregon.

Mike T. Thompson is a Forester, U.S. Department of Agriculture, Forest Service, Rocky Mountain Research Station, Forestry Sciences Laboratory, Ogden, Utah.

Cover: Map of Four Corners facilities, 2007.

Research Highlights

- During calendar year 2007, more than 210.4 million board feet (MMBF) of timber was harvested from Arizona, Colorado, New Mexico, and Utah. Most (55.9 percent) of the harvested volume came from tribal and nonindustrial private timberlands, while 40.9 percent came from National Forests. Ponderosa pine was the leading species harvested for timber in the Four Corners States during 2007, accounting for 34.7 percent of the total. Lodgepole pine accounted for 24.1 percent, followed by spruces and Douglas-fir at 12.9 and 9.1 percent, respectively.

- During 2007, the Four Corners were net importers of timber, with less than 1 percent (983 MBF) of the regional harvest imported for processing from other States. Mills in the Four Corners imported a total of 12.5 MMBF during 2007, while total exports by Four Corners mills were slightly less than 11.6 MMBF.

- Timber-processing capacity (i.e., the volume of timber that could be used by existing timber processors if demand for products were firm and sufficient raw material were available) in the Four Corners during 2007 was approximately 351 MMBF, Scribner. Thus, approximately 60 percent of timber-processing capacity in the region was utilized in 2007.

- This report identified 132 primary timber processing facilities active during 2007 in the Four Corners. These facilities included 62 sawmills, 35 log home or house log manufacturers, 15 log furniture producers, 6 post and pole facilities, 6 viga and latilla producers, and 8 other facilities.

- During 2007, production of lumber and other sawn products exceeded 234 MMBF lumber tally. Lumber production in Arizona was 55 MMBF, Colorado was 116 MMBF, New Mexico was about 40 MMBF, and Utah's lumber production was nearly 23 MMBF.

- Four Corners timber processors produced 259,853 bone dry units (BDU) of residue during 2007, of which just 9,843 BDU (4 percent) went unused. Sawmills generated 233,315 BDU—90 percent of all mill residues in the region.

- The Four Corners primary wood product sales value (f.o.b. the producing mill), including mill residues, totaled nearly $197 million during 2007. A little over $135 million (69 percent) of sales were within the Four Corners States, and 44 percent ($86 million) of all sales were lumber and other sawn products.

Contents

Research Highlights i

Introduction 1
    Four Corners Regional Summary 1
    Historic Overview..2
    Timber Harvest 2
    Timber Flow and Mill Receipts..3
    Forest Products Industry Composition and Operations 5
    Mill Residue: Quantity, Types, and Use 6
    Forest Products Sales and Employment 7

Arizona 8
    Timber Harvest, Flow, and Use...8
    Forest Industry Sectors..15
    Capacity and Utilization 19
    Mill Residue Volumes, Types, and Uses................................19
    Primary Forest Products Markets and Sales 20

Colorado 21
    Timber Harvest, Flow, and Use...22
    Forest Industry Sectors..27
    Capacity and Utilization 32
    Mill Residue Volumes, Types, and Uses................................33
    Primary Forest Products Markets and Sales 33

New Mexico..35
    Timber Harvest, Flow, and Use...35
    Forest Industry Sectors..41
    Capacity and Utilization 45
    Mill Residue Volumes, Types, and Uses................................45
    Primary Forest Products Markets and Sales 46

Utah 47
    Timber Harvest, Flow, and Use...47
    Forest Industry Sectors..52
    Capacity and Utilization 57
    Mill Residue Volumes, Types, and Uses................................57
    Primary Forest Products Markets and Sales 59

References...60

Introduction

This report details timber harvest and describes the composition and operations of the primary forest products industry in the "Four Corners" States (i.e., Arizona, Colorado, New Mexico, and Utah) during calendar year 2007. The report focuses on trends and changes in timber harvest levels in the forest products industry since the 1990s. For historical perspective, some discussion is offered of industry changes throughout the last half of the 20th century.

Timber used in the direct manufacture of products is the focus of this report. Products directly manufactured from timber are referred to as "primary products" and include lumber, posts and poles, house logs, log furniture, vigas and latillas. Reconstituted products made from chipping or grinding timber, as well as products from mill residue (i.e., bark, sawdust, log ends, chips, and planer shavings) generated in the production of primary products, are also included. These reconstituted primary products include excelsior, wood pellets, bark products, and fuelwood. Derivative, or "secondary" products (e.g., window frames, doors, trusses, and furniture) made from primary products are not included in this report.

The major source of data for this report was a census of primary forest products facilities in Arizona, Colorado, New Mexico, and Utah and mills in adjacent States that received timber from the Four Corners States during calendar year 2007. Firms were identified through telephone directories, internet queries, directories of the forest products industries (Lockwood-Post 2008; Random Lengths 2008), and with the assistance of State forestry agencies and the mills themselves. Firms cooperating in the Four Corners census, including out-of-State mills, processed virtually all of the commercial timber harvested from Arizona, Colorado, New Mexico, and Utah in 2007.

This report is the direct result of a cooperative effort between The University of Montana's Bureau of Business and Economic Research (BBER) and the USDA Forest Service, Interior West Forest Inventory and Analysis (IW-FIA) Program. Together, BBER and Forest Service research stations have been conducting periodic mill censuses in the Rocky Mountains for over 30 years. The Forest Industries Data Collection System (FIDACS) was developed by BBER and IW-FIA to collect, compile and make available State- and county-level information on the operations of the forest products industry and the timber it uses. The FIDACS uses a written questionnaire or phone interview of forest products manufacturers to collect the following information for each facility for a given calendar year: production capacity and employment; volume of raw material received by county and ownership; species of timber received; finished product volumes, types, sales values, and market locations; and utilization and marketing of manufacturing residue. Information collected through the FIDACS is processed, analyzed, and stored at the BBER in Missoula, Montana. Additional information is available by request; however, individual firm-level data are confidential and will not be released.

Four Corners Regional Summary

This chapter discusses the Four Corners as a whole, providing a historical overview, as well as information on the forest products industry and timber harvest in 2007. It presents ownership and species composition of harvested timber, types of timber products harvested and processed, as well as movement of timber within the Four Corners and between the region and other States. Timber-processing and

USDA Forest Service Resour. Bull. RMRS-RB-13. 2012

1

production capacities, utilization of mill residues, and forest products sales and employment are also discussed at the regional level.

Historic Overview

Following World War II, with strong housing markets and public policy encouraging timber production on National Forests, timber harvest for industrial products in the Four Corners States increased from about 700 million board feet (MMBF, Scribner log scale) annually during the early 1950s to a peak of approximately 1,000 MMBF in the late 1960s. During the 1970s and 1980s, harvest volumes dropped somewhat with harvest during the late 1980s averaging about 850 MMBF annually. Timber harvest from the region declined dramatically during the 1990s, caused largely by decreases in the harvest from National Forests. National Forest timber harvests in Arizona, Colorado, New Mexico, and Utah followed the course of most Western States, declining due to threatened and endangered species, appeals and litigation directed at Federal timber sales, and lower Federal budget levels.

In Arizona and New Mexico, the listing of the Mexican spotted owl had a profound downward impact on National Forest timber harvest levels. The Mexican spotted owl was listed as threatened by the United States Fish and Wildlife Service in March of 1993. In August of 1995, a Federal judge enjoined the logging of new timber sales on National Forests in Arizona and New Mexico pending development of a recovery plan for the owl (Silver and others v. Thomas and others 1995). Between 1990 and 1996, harvest from Arizona National Forests dropped from 300 MMBF annually to about 28 MMBF, and harvest from New Mexico National Forests fell from about 125 MMBF to less than 20 MMBF annually. Most of the material harvested during the period was for fuelwood, not industrial timber products. The lifting of the injunction in December 1996 resulted in increases in National Forest timber offerings in 1997 and 1998. The cut from Arizona National Forests increased to about 61 MMBF in 1997 and 63 MMBF in 1998; the cut from New Mexico National Forests increased slightly to 23 MMBF in 1997 and 30 MMBF in 1998.

Declines in National Forest timber offerings have negatively impacted both Colorado's and Utah's industry as well, leading to substantially lower total harvest. Though not as sharp nor abrupt as in Arizona and New Mexico, reductions in National Forest timber harvest have significantly accelerated closures and have yielded very low levels of capacity utilization at sawmills—the largest timber processing sector in the two States—and played a part in the closure of the two oriented strand board (OSB) operations in Colorado. The actual number of timber processors in the two States decreased from approximately 182 facilities during 2002 to 91 facilities in 2007. Decreases in facilities occurred in all sectors but most conspicuously in the log home and log furniture industries, where Colorado ranked second behind Montana in 2002, with Utah fourth in value of output from log home plants in the Western United States.

Timber Harvest

Harvest volumes presented in this report for calendar year 2007 came from the FIDACS census of Four Corners and out-of-State mills receiving timber harvested from the region. When available, similar timber harvest characterizations for the individual States (Arizona, Colorado, New Mexico, and Utah) were used

Table 4C-1: Four Corners timber harvest by ownership class, 2002 and 2007 (source: Morgan and others 2006).

Ownership class	2002		2007	
	MBF Scribner	Percentage of harvest	MBF Scribner	Percentage of harvest
Private and tr bal timberland	234,456	72.5	117,708	55.9
Tribal	*134,840*	*41.7*	*23,714*	*11.3*
Private	*99,616*	*30.8*	*93,994*	*44.7*
Public timberland	89,105	27.5	92,700	44.1
National Forest	*84,536*	*26.1*	*86,036*	*40.9*
Other public	*4,569*	*1.4*	*6,664*	*3.2*
All owners	323,561	100	210,408	100

for comparison. Periodic State-level reports (Wilson and Spencer 1967; Setzer and Wilson 1970; Setzer 1971 a,b; Green and Setzer 1974; Setzer and Barrett 1977; Setzer and Shupe 1977; Setzer and Throssell 1977a,b; McLain 1985; McLain 1988; McLain 1989; Keegan and others 1995; Keegan and others 2001a,b; Morgan and others 2006) provided the bulk of historic timber harvest information. Published timber harvest reports for recent years were not available, with the exception of Bureau of Land Management (BLM) forest products offerings and USDA Forest Service annual "cut and sold" reports. Small differences may exist between the numbers reported here and those in BLM and Forest Service reports. These differences are due to varying reporting units and conversion factors, rounding error, scaling discrepancies between sellers and buyers, and other reporting variations.

During calendar year 2007, more than 210.4 MMBF of timber was harvested from Arizona, Colorado, New Mexico, and Utah. This harvest volume represents less than 0.1 percent of the approximately 169.5 billion board feet of sawtimber inventory on nonreserved timberlands in the four States (U.S. Department of Agriculture, FIDO 2009). Timber harvested from Four Corners timberland and manufactured into wood products came from three broad ownership classes: tribal lands, nonindustrial private forest (NIPF) land, and public lands. Most (55.9 percent) of the harvested volume came from tribal and NIPF timberlands, while 40.9 percent came from National Forests (table 4C-1). Ponderosa pine was the leading species harvested for timber in the Four Corners States during 2007, accounting for 34.7 percent of the total (table 4C-2). Lodgepole pine accounted for 24.1 percent, followed by aspen and spruces at 13.3 and 12.9 percent, respectively. Sawlogs were the leading component of the timber harvest in the Four Corners (table 4C-3); at 83 percent, no other product type came close in harvested volume. Trees harvested for fiber logs and industrial fuelwood contributed 7.2 percent to the total, while house logs accounted for 5.9 percent of the harvest.

Timber Flow and Mill Receipts

During 2007, the Four Corners were net importers of timber, with less than one-half percent (964 MBF) of the regional harvest imported for processing (table 4C-4). Of this imported volume, over 81 percent (almost 781 MBF) was house logs. There was some volume traded and utilized between the States in the Four Corners region, but no identifiable volume was exported from the Four Corners States for processing in 2007. By ownership, timber from private lands was imported in the largest volumes, with timber from National Forest next. This flow of

USDA Forest Service Resour. Bull. RMRS-RB-13. 2012

3

Table 4C-2: Four Corners timber harvest by species, 2002 and 2007 (source: Morgan and others 2006).

Species	2002		2007	
	MBF Scribner	Percentage of harvest	MBF Scribner	Percentage of harvest
Ponderosa pine	186,955	57.8	73,041	34.7
Lodgepole pine	21,822	6.7	50,648	24.1
Aspen	20,399	6.3	28,088	13.3
Spruces	46,850	14.5	27,057	12.9
Douglas-fir	30,165	9.3	19,065	9.1
Firs	16,882	5.2	12,351	5.9
Other species[a]	489	0.2	158	0.1
All species	323,562	100	210,408	100

[a]Other species include juniper, other softwoods, and hardwoods other than aspen.

Table 4C-3: Four Corners timber harvest by product, 2002 and 2007 (source: Morgan and others 2006).

Product	2002		2007	
	MBF Scribner	Percentage of harvest	MBF Scribner	Percentage of harvest
Sawlogs	279,317	86.3	174,629	83.0
Fiber logs and industrial fuelwood	14,763	4.6	15,144	7.2
House logs	20,695	6.4	12,495	5.9
Posts and poles	4,104	1.3	5,497	2.6
Vigas	3,655	1.1	2,368	1.1
Other products[a]	1,029	0.3	275	0.1
All products	323,562	100	210,408	100

[a]Other products include furniture logs, pilings, and utility poles.

Table 4C-4: Four Corners timber products imports and exports[a], 2007.

Timber product	Imports	Exports	Net imports (net exports)
	---Thousand board feet, Scribner---		
Sawlogs	3,536	3,431	105
House logs	2,220	1,445	775
Other products[b]	6,747	6,644	103
All products	12,503	11,520	983

[a] Imports and exports are with other States and North American countries.

[b]Other products include post and poles, fiber logs, firewood, furniture logs, vigas and industrial fuel wood.

timber into the region created a difference in the volume of timber harvested from the Four Corners and the volume received by the region's mills. The large majority of timber used by primary forest products firms in the Four Corners came from within the four-State region. Additional volume came from Idaho, Montana, and Oregon, with some smaller volumes from Wyoming and Canada.

While the 2007 harvest exceeded 210.4 MMBF, total receipts by Four Corners mills were slightly more than 211 MMBF, a volume equivalent to 101 percent

Table 4C-5: Timber received by the Four Corners primary forest products industry by ownership class and product, 2007.

Ownership class	Sawlogs	Fuelwood/ bioenergy	House logs	Post/pole	Other products[b]	All products
			-------------Thousand board feet, Scribner-------------			
Private and tribal timberland	104,270	2,402	3,089	1,942	6,473	118,175
Private	*82,940*	*802*	*2,680*	*1,567*	*6,473*	*94,461*
Tribal	*21,330*	*1,600*	*409*	*375*	*-*	*23,714*
Public timberland	70,463	3,625	10,182	3,555	5,391	93,216
National Forest	*67,826*	*3,625*	*10,114*	*2,430*	*2,492*	*86,487*
Other owners[a]	*2,637*	*-*	*68*	*1,125*	*2,899*	*6,729*
All owners	174,734	6,027	13,271	5,497	11,863	211,391
			-------------Percentage of product by ownership-------------			
Private and tribal timberland	59.7	39.9	23.3	35.3	54.6	55.9
Private	*47.5*	*13.3*	*20.2*	*28.5*	*54.6*	*44.7*
Tribal	*12.2*	*26.5*	*3.1*	*6.8*	*-*	*11.2*
Public timberland	40.3	60.1	76.7	64.7	45.4	44.1
National Forest	*38.8*	*60.1*	*76.2*	*44.2*	*21.0*	*40.9*
Other owners[a]	*1.5*	*-*	*0.5*	*20.5*	*24.4*	*3.2*
All owners	82.7	2.9	6.3	2.6	5.6	100

[a]Other owners include other public ownerships and Canadian imports.

[b]Other products include logs for log furniture, vigas, latillas, and fiber logs.

of the harvest. Sawlogs accounted for the vast majority (83 percent) of timber received by Four Corners mills (table 4C-5), followed by house logs (6 percent). The NIPF landowners supplied the largest share (45 percent) of timber received by mills in the four States, followed by National Forest System (NFS) lands (41 percent) and then tribal owners (11 percent). Timber-processing capacity (the volume of timber that could be used by existing timber processors if demand for products were firm and sufficient raw material were available) in the Four Corners during 2007 was approximately 351 MMBF, Scribner. Thus, approximately 60 percent of timber-processing capacity in the region was utilized in 2007.

Forest Products Industry Composition and Operations

The FIDACS census identified 132 primary timber processing facilities active during 2007 in the Four Corners. These facilities included 62 sawmills, 35 log home or house log manufacturers, 15 log furniture producers, 6 post and pole facilities, 6 viga and latilla producers, and 8 other facilities. Colorado and Utah had the most facilities and the largest shares of the log home and log furniture sectors. Arizona and New Mexico had fewer facilities but more of the viga and latilla sector.

Primary timber processors in the Four Corners produced an array of products including: dimension lumber, board and shop lumber, mine timbers, railroad ties, pallet stock, dunnage, excelsior, posts, poles, vigas, latillas, finished house logs, log homes, and log furniture, as well as wood pellets, fuelwood, bark, mulch, and pulp chips from mill residues. During 2007, production of lumber and other sawn products exceeded 233.7 MMBF lumber tally. State contributions included Colorado (116 MMBF), Arizona (55 MMBF), New Mexico (40 MMBF), and Utah (23 MMBF). Production of house logs, vigas, and latillas totaled more than

USDA Forest Service Resour. Bull. RMRS-RB-13. 2012

5

5.4 million lineal feet (MMLF), and more than 2.3 million pieces of log furniture, and posts and poles were produced by facilities in the Four Corners.

Mill Residue: Quantity, Types, and Use

A substantial portion of the wood fiber, including bark processed by primary forest product plants, ends up as mill residue. Three types of wood residues are typically generated by the primary wood products industry: coarse or chippable residue consisting of edging, slabs, trim, log ends, and pieces of veneer; fine residue consisting primarily of planer shavings and sawdust; and bark. The 2007 census collected information on volumes and uses of mill residue. Actual residue volumes, reported in bone-dry units (BDU), were obtained from facilities that sold all or most of their residues. All mills reported how their residues were used on a percentage basis. One BDU is the equivalent of 2,400 pounds of oven-dry wood.

Four Corners timber processors produced 259,853 BDUs of residue during 2007, of which just 9,843 BDUs (3.8 percent) went unused (table 4C-6). Coarse residues were the region's largest residue component (55 percent of all residues), with just over 2 percent going unused. About 40 percent of coarse residue was used by the pulp and board sector, 35 percent went to the energy sector, and an additional 23 percent went to other uses. Fine residue made up the second largest component (28 percent) in 2007, with sawdust comprising 18.5 percent and shavings 9.4 percent. All but 5,140 BDUs (7 percent) of fine residue were used, primarily as animal bedding and mulch. Four Corners facilities generated 44,087 BDUs of bark while processing timber in 2007, of which all but 3 percent was utilized. About 55 percent of bark was used as mulch, while 23 percent went to energy. During 2007, sawmills generated 233,315 BDUs—90 percent of all mill residues in the region. Residue volume factors, which express mill residue generated per unit of lumber produced, were derived from production and residue output volumes provided by mills (table 4C-7).

Table 4C-6: Production and disposition of Four Corners mill residues, 2007.

Residue type	Total utilized	Pulp and board	Energy	Mulch/bedding	Unspecified use	Unused	Total produced
				Bone-dry units[a]			
Coarse	140,066	57,300	50,062	-	32,704	3,323	143,389
Fine	67,237	-	22,512	42,281	2,444	5,140	72,377
Sawdust	*43,222*	*-*	*16,005*	*25,195*	*2,022*	*4,856*	*48,078*
Planer shavings	*24,015*	*-*	*6,507*	*17,086*	*422*	*284*	*24,299*
Bark	42,707	-	10,213	24,107	8,387	1,380	44,087
All residues	250,010	57,300	82,787	66,388	43,535	9,843	259,853
				Percentage of residue type by use			
Coarse	97.7	40.0	34.9	0.0	22.8	2.3	55.2
Fine	92.9	0.0	31.1	58.4	3.4	7.1	27.9
Sawdust	*89.9*	*0.0*	*33.3*	*52.4*	*4.2*	*10.1*	*18.5*
Planer shavings	*98.8*	*0.0*	*26.8*	*70.3*	*1.7*	*1.2*	*9.4*
Bark	96.9	0.0	23.2	54.7	19.0	3.1	17.0
All residues	96.2	22.1	31.9	25.5	16.8	3.8	100

[a]Bone-dry unit = 2,400 lb oven-dry wood.

Table 4C-7: Four Corners sawmill residue factors, 2002 and 2007 (source: Morgan and others 2006).

Type of residue	2002 BDU per MBF	2007 BDU per MBF
Coarse	0.56	0.56
Sawdust	0.19	0.19
Planer shavings	0.16	0.10
Bark	0.28	0.17
Total	1.19	1.02

[a]Bone-dry unit (BDU = 2,400 lb oven-dry wood) of residue generated for every 1,000 board feet of lumber manufactured.

Forest Products Sales and Employment

Mills responding to the FIDACS survey summarized their calendar year 2007 shipments of finished wood products, providing information on volume, sales value, and geographic destination. Mills usually distributed their products either through their own distribution channels or through independent wholesalers and selling agents. Because of subsequent transactions, the geographic destination reported here may not reflect the final delivery points of shipments.

The Four Corners primary wood product sales value (f.o.b. the producing mill), including mill residues, totaled nearly $197 million during 2007 (table 4C-8). A little over $135 million (69 percent) of these sales were within the Four Corners States, and 44 percent ($86 million) of all sales were lumber and other sawn products. Other products, which include excelsior, firewood, and mill residue, accounted for $50 million (25.6 percent of total sales). Colorado led the region with more than $104 million in sales, of which approximately $30 million came from the other products sector. Total sales for Arizona, New Mexico, and Utah ranged from $26 to $38 million for each State (tables A18, N17, U16).

While the forest products industry continues to provide substantial employment opportunities in the Southwest, the number of workers has declined radically over the past 5 years. Forest products firms, including logging companies, employed about 2,700 people in the Four Corners area in 2007, compared to 3,800 in 2002. Of this total, approximately 1,000 individuals were employed in logging in 2007 (5.0 workers per MMBF harvested), compared to 1,600 in 2002 (QCEW 2004, 2007; REIS 2004, 2007). Primary timber processing facilities employed 1,700 workers in 2007 (8.3 workers per MMBF consumed) vs. 2,200 in 2002.

USDA Forest Service Resour. Bull. RMRS-RB-13. 2012

7

Table 4C-8: Destination and sales value of Four Corners primary wood products and mill residues, 2007.

Product	Within 4-Corner States	Other Rocky Mtn States[a]	Far West[b]	Northeast[c]	South[d]	North Central[e]	Mexico, Canada, or other[f]	Total
				Thousand 2007 dollars				
Lumber, mine timbers, and other sawn products	68,159	3,554	1,280	139	3,371	5,236	4,547	86,286
House logs and log homes	25,463	1,656	504	862	6,604	1,347	40	36,476
Posts, poles, vigas, latillas, and log furniture	16,192	1,985	1,765	1,166	1,374	1,111	-	23,593
Other products[g]	25,396	2,924	7,245	386	8,328	3,881	2,186	50,346
Total	135,210	10,119	10,794	2,553	19,677	11,575	6,773	$196,701
				Percentage of regional sales by product				
Lumber, mine timbers, and other sawn products	50.4	35.1	11.9	5.4	17.1	45.2	67.1	43.9
House logs and log homes	18.8	16.4	4.7	33.8	33.6	11.6	0.6	18.5
Posts, poles, vigas, latillas, and log furniture	12.0	19.6	16.4	45.7	7.0	9.6	-	12.0
Other products[g]	18.8	28.9	67.1	15.1	42.3	33.5	32.3	25.6
Total	68.7	5.1	5.5	1.3	10.0	5.9	3.4	100

[a]Other Rocky Mountains includes Idaho, Montana, Nevada.

[b]Far West includes Alaska, California, Hawaii, Oregon, and Washington.

[c]Northeast includes Connecticut, Maine, Massachusetts, New Hampshire, New Jersey, New York, Pennsylvania, Rhode Island, and Vermont.

[d]South includes Alabama, Arkansas, Delaware, Florida, Georgia, Kentucky, Louisiana, Maryland, Mississippi, North Carolina, Oklahoma, South Carolina, Tennessee, Texas, Virginia, and West Virginia.

[e]North Central includes Illinois, Indiana, Iowa, Kansas, Michigan, Minnesota, Missouri, Nebraska, North Dakota, Ohio, South Dakota, and Wisconsin.

[f]Other areas consist of products being shipped outside the United States.

[g]Other products include excelsior, mill residues, mulch, and fuel pellets; they do not include paper products.

Arizona

This chapter reviews Arizona's 2007 timber harvest and forest products industry activities and changes that occurred since the 2002 industry census conducted by Morgan and others (2006). Details of timber harvest, flow, and use are followed by descriptions of the primary processing sectors, capacity and utilization statistics, and mill residue characteristics. The chapter concludes with information on primary wood products industry sales by Arizona mills.

Timber Harvest, Flow, and Use

In 2007, Arizona had approximately 3.4 million acres of nonreserved timberland (U.S. Department of Agriculture, FIDO 2009), with National Forests accounting for 71 percent, private and tribal owners accounting for 28 percent, and other public agencies accounting for the remaining 1 percent (table A1). All private timberland

Table A1: Arizona nonreserved timberland by ownership class (source: Forest Inventory and Analysis Program, 2008).

Ownership class	Thousand acres	Percentage of nonreserved timberland
National Forest	2,395	71
Private and tr bal	959	28
Other public	31	1
Total	3,385	100

was classified as NIPF timberland. With the exception of several Native American tribes, Arizona had no large tracts of timberland owned by entities operating primary wood processing facilities. Sawtimber volume on nonreserved timberlands was estimated at 5.3 billion cubic feet or approximately 29.8 billion board feet Scribner in 2008 (U.S. Department of Agriculture, FIDO 2009).

Timber Harvest

Arizona's 2007 timber harvest was 53.8 MMBF Scribner, only 42 percent of the 2002 harvest, and about 15 percent of the annual harvest during the late 1980s (Keegan and others 2001a). The decline in Arizona's total annual timber harvest since 1990 was largely due to the decline in National Forest timber harvest. The major factor that contributed to the harvest increase from 1998 to 2002 was the salvage of 90 MMBF of dead, mostly fire-killed timber, accounting for 70 percent of the 2002 harvest volume. In 1998 dead trees accounted for just 3 percent (2.4 MMBF) of the total harvest. Although substantial acreages of both public and tribal forests burned between 1998 and 2002, tribal landowners were able to respond relatively quickly and harvested over 82 MMBF of fire-killed timber in 2002. Once the areas affected by the large fires were salvaged, the annual harvest fell to below pre-fire levels.

As National Forest and total timber harvest in the State declined, a disproportionate and diminishing share of Arizona's timber harvest came from National Forest timberlands in recent years (table A2). In 1966, 1974, and 1984 National Forests accounted for 60 percent or more of harvested volume (Setzer and Throssell 1977a; McLain 1988), whereas in 2002 and 2007 National Forests accounted for 16 and 40 percent of harvest volume, respectively (Morgan and others 2006). National Forests provided the majority (93 percent) of house logs harvested in 2007, but tribal and NIPF landowners provided the majority of sawlogs and other products

Table A2: Proportion of Arizona timber harvest by ownership class, selected years (sources: Setzer 1971; Setzer and Throssell 1977; McLain 1988; Keegan and others 2001a; Morgan and others 2006).

Ownership class	1966	1974	1984	1998	2002	2007
	----------Percentage of harvest------------					
Private and tribal timberland	25.0	41.0	33.5	63.0	84.4	59.0
Private	*1.0*	*-*	*33.5*	*3.0*	*1.6*	*51.0*
Tribal	*24.0*	*41.0*	*-*	*60.0*	*82.8*	*8.0*
Public timberland	75.0	59.0	66.5	37.0	15.6	41.0
National Forest	*75.0*	*59.0*	*66.2*	*37.0*	*15.6*	*40.0*
Other public	*-*	*-*	*0.3*	*-*	*-*	*1.0*
All owners	100	100	100	100	100	100

USDA Forest Service Resour. Bull. RMRS-RB-13. 2012

9

Table A3: Arizona timber products harvested by ownership class, 2007.

Ownership class	Sawlogs	House logs	Other products[a]	All products
	---------------Thousand board feet, Scribner-----------------			
Private timberland	26,830	20	444	27,294
National Forest	21,141	407	175	21,723
Tribal timberland	2,800	10	1,600	4,410
State	350	-	-	350
All owners	51,121	437	2,219	53,777
	---Percentage of harvested product by ownership---			
Private timberland	52.5	4.6	20.0	50.8
National Forest	41.4	93.1	7.9	40.4
Tribal timberland	5.5	2.3	72.1	8.2
State	0.7	-	-	0.7
All owners	95.1	0.8	4.1	100

[a]Other products include industrial fuelwood, furniture logs, fiber logs, and viga logs.

(table A3). Sawlogs accounted for 95 percent (51 MMBF) of the total volume harvested.

Historically, 80 percent or more of the State's annual timber harvest came from three counties: Apache, Coconino, and Navajo. In 2007, Apache County led Arizona's timber harvest with 59 percent of total volume. Coconino County followed with 27 percent (table A4). In 2002 Navajo led with 50 percent followed by Gila and then Coconino County (Morgan and others 2006). In 1984, Apache led followed by Coconino and Navajo (McLain 1988). In 1974, Coconino County led the State with almost 38 percent of the harvest, followed by Navajo with 34 percent and Apache with 19 percent (Setzer and Throssell 1977a). Similarly, Coconino County was the largest timber producer in 1969, contributing 32 percent of the harvest, followed by Apache and Navajo with 25 and 23 percent, respectively (Setzer 1971a).

Table A4: Arizona timber harvest by county, selected years (sources: McLain 1988; Keegan and others 2001a; Morgan and others 2006).

County	1984	1998	2002	2007	1984	1998	2002	2007
	---MBF Scribner---				-------Percentage-------			
Apache	171,128	15,641	6,350	31,610	44.7	20.5	5.0	58.8
Coconino	150,727	15,314	14,889	14,353	39.4	20.1	11.6	26.7
Gila	931	5,405	39,960	1,960	0.2	7.1	31.2	3.6
Graham	-	-	1,100	1,100	-	-	0.9	2.0
Greenlee	4,623	1,515	-	-	1.2	2.0	-	-
Maricopa	-	-	-	0	-	-	-	[a]
Navajo	52,745	38,384	64,027	3,094	13.8	50.3	49.9	5.8
Pima	-	33	-	-	-	[a]	-	-
Santa Cruz	-	-	-	48	-	-	-	0.1
Yavapai	2,220	20	1,895	1,612	0.6	[a]	1.5	3.0
Total[b]	382,674	76,312	128,220	53,777	100	100	100	100

[a]Less than 0.05 percent.

[b]Percentage detail may not sum to 100% due to rounding.

Table A5: Proportion of Arizona timber harvest by species, selected years (sources: Setzer 1971; Setzer and Throssell 1977; McLain 1988; Keegan and others 2001a; Morgan and others 2006).

Species	1969[a]	1974[a]	1984	1998	2002	2007
				Percentage of harvest		
Ponderosa pine	74.2	69.6	90.6	87.5	94.8	86.4
Engelmann spruce	0.9	2.1	2.3	3.1	1.2	5.5
Dougles-fir	5.3	5.6	4.5	6.9	2.4	3.6
White fir	3.6	4.8	2.4	1.3	1.5	3.1
Pinyon pine, juniper, limber pine, aspen	16.0	17.9	0.2	1.2	< 0.05	1.4
All species[b]	100	100	100	100	100	100

[a]Harvest data for 1969 and 1974 include fuelwood; 1984, 1998, 2002, 2007 do not include fuelwood.

[b]Percentage detail may not add to 100 due to rounding.

Table A6: Arizona timber harvest by species, selected years (sources: McLain 1988; Keegan and others 2001a; Morgan and others 2006).

Species	1984	1998	2002	2007
		MBF Scribner		
Ponderosa pine	346,851	66,804	121,614	46,483
Engelmann spruce	8,667	2,340	1,551	2,948
Douglas-fir	17,217	5,264	3,129	1,915
White fir	9,214	961	1,900	1,662
Other species[a]	722	943	26	769
All species[b]	382,674	76,312	128,220	53,777

[a]Other species include juniper, other softwoods, and hardwoods.

[b]May not sum due to rounding.

Ponderosa pine continued to be the leading species harvested among all product types in Arizona in 2007 (table A7), accounting for 86 percent of total harvest (table A5). Douglas-fir, white and subalpine firs, and Engelmann spruce were harvested in relatively small quantities (table A6). Engelmann spruce comprised only 17 percent of the 2007 house log harvest, Ponderosa pine harvest spiked in 2002 at 95 percent of total harvest partly because of the salvage of fire- and beetle-killed ponderosa pine (Morgan and others 2006). In 1984, ponderosa pine accounted for more than 90 percent of the harvest (347 MMBF of 383 MMBF harvested), but McLain (1988) reported that live trees accounted for 97 percent of this volume.

Timber Flow

The majority (97 percent) of Arizona's 2007 timber harvest was processed in State. However, Arizona was a net exporter of timber. Slightly more than 1.7 MMBF was exported for processing in Colorado, Nevada, and Utah, while a very small amount of timber was imported from Montana, Oregon, and Utah for processing in Arizona (table A8).

Timber processors in Arizona received 52,133 MBF of timber in 2007. Ownership sources of timber delivered to Arizona mills in 2007 varied slightly with more volume coming from National Forest land than in 2002. More than 60 percent of all receipts came from private and tribal timberlands with a little less than 40 percent from National Forests (table A9), which supplied timber to 11 Arizona mills (65 percent) in 2007. National Forests provided Arizona log home manufacturers with 96 percent of the house log volume processed in Arizona, with NIPF landowners providing the remaining 4 percent (table A10).

USDA Forest Service Resour. Bull. RMRS-RB-13. 2012

11

Table A7: Arizona timber harvest by species and product, 2007.

Species	Sawlogs	House logs	Other products[b]	All products
	---------------Thousand board feet, Scribner------------------			
Ponderosa pine	43,955	331	2,197	46,483
Engelmann spruce	2,874	75	-	2,949
Douglas-fir	1,912	3	-	1,915
True firs[a]	1,661	-	-	1,661
Other species[c]	719	28	22	769
All species	51,121	437	2,219	53,777
	---------------Percentage of product by species-------------			
Ponderosa pine	86.0	75.7	99.0	86.4
Engelmann spruce	5.6	17.2	-	5.5
Douglas-fir	3.7	0.7	-	3.6
True firs[a]	3.2	-	-	3.1
Other species[c]	1.4	6.4	1.0	1.4
All species	95.1	0.8	4.1	100

[a]True firs include white and subalpine fir.

[b]Other products include industrial fuelwood, furniture logs, fiber logs, and viga logs.

[c]Other species include juniper,other softwoods, and hardwoods.

Table A8: Arizona timber products imports and exports, 2007.

Timber product	Imports	Exports	Net imports (net exports)
	---Thousand board feet, Scribner---		
Sawlogs	-	1,683	(1,683)
House logs	50	35	15
Other products[a]	24	-	24
All products	74	1,718	(1,644)

[a]Other products include furniture logs, fiber logs, and viga logs.

Table A9: Ownership of timber products received by Arizona forest products industry, 1998, 2002 and 2007 (source: Keegan and others 2001a; Morgan and others 2006).

Ownership class	1998 MBF Scribner	1998 Percentage of total	2002 MBF Scribner	2002 Percentage of total	2007 MBF Scribner	2007 Percentage of total
Private and tribal timberland	48,102	71.1	58,108	76.3	31,706	60.8
Tribal	45,964	68.0	56,150	73.8	4,400	8.4
Private	2,138	3.2	1,958	2.6	27,306	52.4
National Forests	19,510	28.9	18,006	23.7	20,427	39.2
All owners	67,612	100	76,114	100	52,133	100

Table A10: Timber received by Arizona forest products industry by ownership class and product, 2007.

Ownership class	Sawlogs	House logs	Other products[a]	All products
	---------------Thousand board feet, Scribner---------------			
Private and tribal timberland	29,630	20	2,056	31,706
Private	*26,830*	*20*	*456*	*27,306*
Tribal	*2,800*	*-*	*1,600*	*4,400*
Public timberland	19,808	432	187	20,427
National Forest	*19,808*	*432*	*187*	*20,427*
All owners	49,438	452	2,243	52,133
	--------------Percentage of product by owner-------------			
Private and tribal timberland	59.9	4.4	91.7	60.8
Private	*54.3*	*4.4*	*20.3*	*52.4*
Tribal	*5.7*	*-*	*71.3*	*8.4*
Public timberland	40.1	95.6	8.3	39.2
National Forest	*40.1*	*95.6*	*8.3*	*39.2*
All owners	94.8	0.9	4.3	100

[a]Other products include industrial fuelwood, furniture logs, fiber logs, and viga logs.

Timber Use

Arizona's 2007 timber harvest—approximately 11,300 thousand cubic feet (MCF), exclusive of bark (fig. A1)—was used by several manufacturing sectors both within and outside Arizona. Of this volume, 9,113 MCF was delivered as logs to sawmills, 73 MCF went to log home manufacturers, and 2,114 MCF went to other plants, including post, pole, viga, latilla, and wood pellet manufacturers, as well as residue-utilizing facilities including bioenergy facilities, pulp mills, reconstituted board plants, and mulch and animal bedding producers. Volumes are presented in cubic feet rather than board feet Scribner because both mill residues and timber products are displayed.

The following conversion factors were used to convert Scribner board foot volume to cubic feet:

- 5.98 board feet per cubic foot for house logs;
- 5.61 board feet per cubic foot for sawlogs;
- 1.05 board foot per cubic foot for all other products.

Of the 9,113 MCF of timber received by sawmills, 3,672 MCF (40 percent) was processed into finished lumber or other sawn products, and about 182 MCF was lost to shrinkage. The remaining 5,259 MCF (58 percent) yielded mill residue. About 5,198 MCF of sawmill residue was utilized by other sectors within Arizona and in other States—1,455 MCF for biomass energy; and 3,743 MCF for pulp, livestock bedding, or mulch. Only 61 MCF (<1 percent) of sawmill residue remained unused. Of the 73 MCF of timber received by log home manufacturers, 31 MCF (43 percent) became house logs. The remaining 42 MCF became mill residue. About 8 MCF of house log residue was used by other sectors; and about 34 MCF remained unused. Of the 2,114 MCF of timber received by other manufacturers, all was utilized for solid wood products such as posts, vigas, or latillas, or used in residue-related products like mulch, livestock bedding, fuel pellets, or for biomass energy production.

USDA Forest Service Resour. Bull. RMRS-RB-13. 2012

13

Arizona Timber Harvest and Flow, 2007

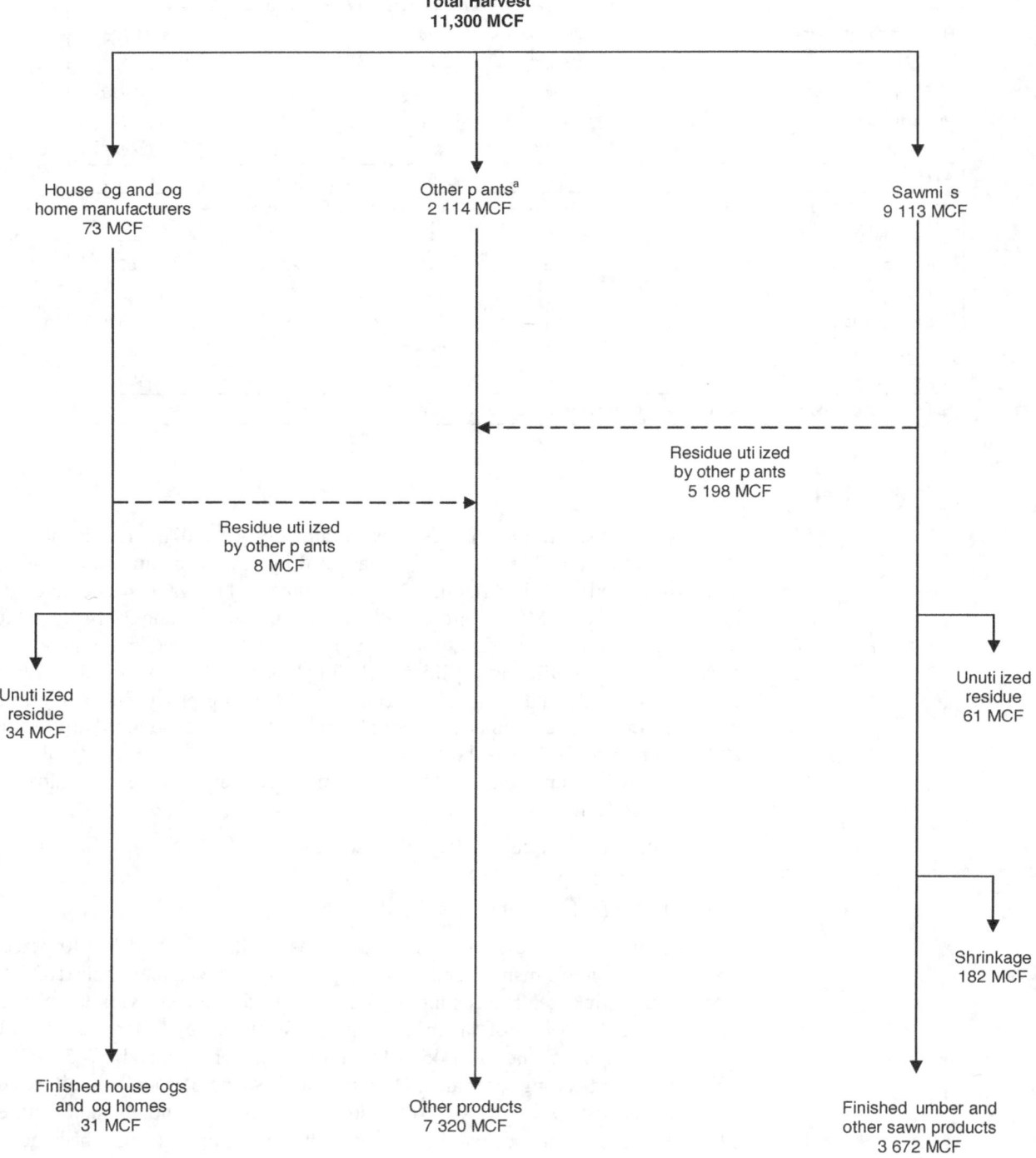

Figure A1: Arizona timber harvest and flow, 2007.

Forest Industry Sectors

Arizona's primary forest products industry in 2007 consisted of 17 active manufacturers in six counties (table A11). Facilities tended to be located near the forest resource along the northern side of the Mogollon Plateau, with concentrations in southern Apache and Navajo counties (fig. A2). The sawmill sector, manufacturing lumber and other sawn products, was the largest sector operating in 2007 with 8 facilities—three less than were operating in 2002. Five facilities produced house logs and log homes, the same as reported in 2002. A viga and latilla manufacturer, a log furniture producer, one bark producer, and a fuel pellet manufacturer were also actively purchasing or utilizing timber in 2007. These four firms were indicative of the increased diversity of timber-processors that developed in Arizona since the end of the 1980s. One paper mill utilizing recycled material also operated in Arizona during 2007 but did not receive any timber or mill residue. As recently as 1998 this facility used some roundwood pulpwood and mill residues and was included in previous reports (McLain 1988; Keegan and others 2001a).

Primary wood products sales increased as did the variety of producers since 2002, with finished product sales in 2007 about 5 percent higher than in 2002 (table A12). The 2007 sales increase over 2002, however, did not occur in the sawmill industry, but in the more recently developing log home and other products

Table A11: Active Arizona primary wood products facilities by county and product, 2007 (sources: McLain 1988; Keegan and others 2001a; Morgan and others 2006).

County	Lumber	Log homes and house logs	Other products[a]	Pulp and paper	Total
Apache	1	1			2
Coconino		2			2
Gila	1				1
Maricopa	3		1		4
Navajo	1	1	3		5
Yavapai	2	1			3
2007 Total	**8**	**5**	**4**	**0**	**17**
2002 Total	11	5	7	0	23
1998 Total	6	4	2	1	13
1990 Total	14	3	1	1	19
1984 Total	20	0	2	1	23

[a]Other products include posts, poles, vigas, latillas, fuel pellets, log furniture, and biomass energy.

Table A12: Finished product sales of Arizona's primary wood products sectors, selected years. (sources: WWPA various years; Keegan and others 2001a; Morgan and others 2006).

Sector	1984	1990	1998	2002	2007
	--------Thousands of 2007 dollars--------				
Sawmills	$176,934	$144,784	$30,640	$27,677	$20,458
Log home and other sectors[a]	248	570	2,393	7,193	16,076
Total[b]	$177,182	$145,354	$33,033	$34,870	$36,534

[a]Other sectors include producers of posts, poles, vigas, latillas, log furniture, and fuel pellets.

[b]All sales are reported F.O.B. the manufacturer's plant. Sales of mill residues, mulch, and paper not included for comparison to previous years.

USDA Forest Service Resour. Bull. RMRS-RB-13. 2012

15

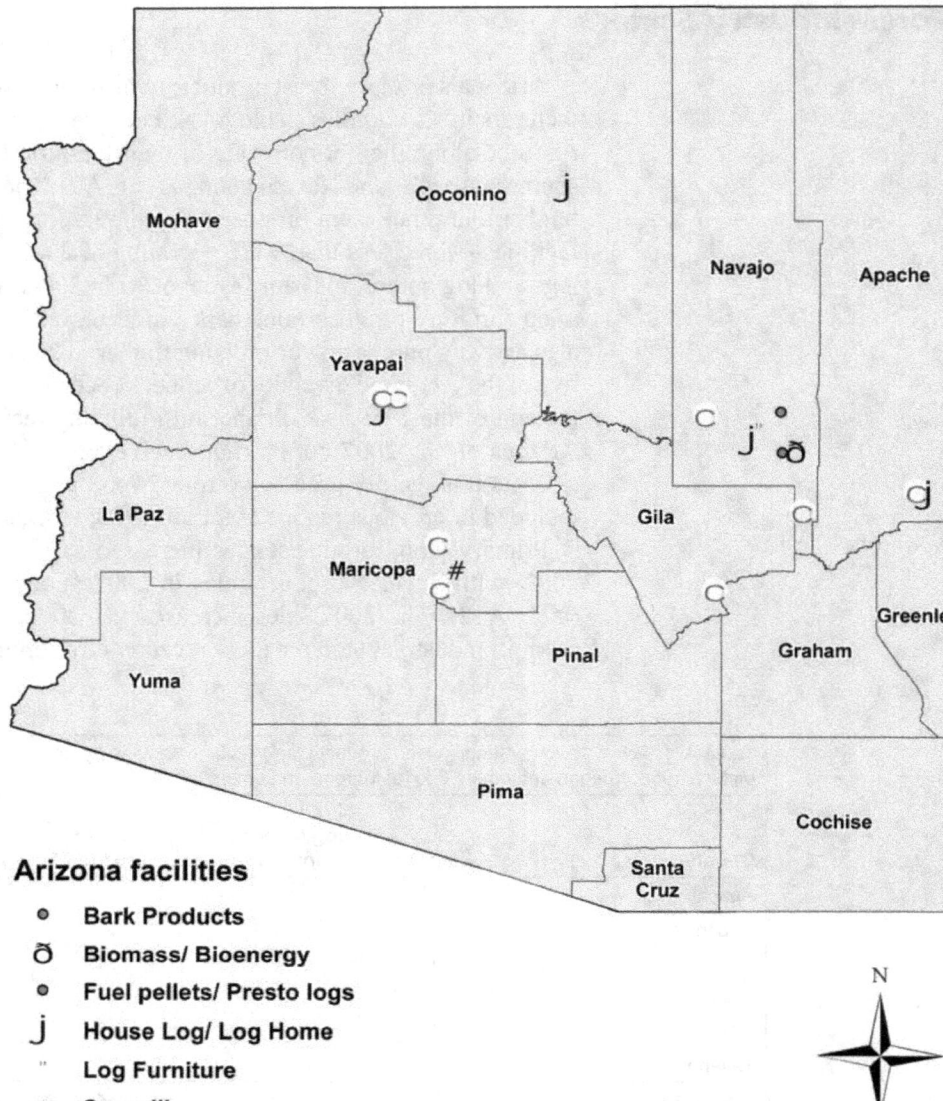

Figure A2: Map of Arizona facilities.

Arizona facilities

- ◉ Bark Products
- ᵭ Biomass/ Bioenergy
- ◉ Fuel pellets/ Presto logs
- j House Log/ Log Home
- ˮ Log Furniture
- C Sawmill
- # Vigas/ Latillas

sectors where sales increased 572 percent since 1998. In 1990, the four firms manufacturing products other than lumber accounted for only $570,000, less than 0.5 percent of total wood products sales that year (Keegan and others 2001a). In 2007, sales from the house log and other products manufacturers exceeded $16 million, and accounted for 44 percent of finished products sales.

Sawmill Sector

The number of sawmills in Arizona decreased in the past five years by over 25 percent, while total lumber production decreased by 34 percent from about 83 MMBF in 2002 to less than 55 MMBF in 2007 (table A13). A number of the State's largest sawmills closed between 1998 and 2007, shifting a larger proportion of the State's lumber production into small mills producing less than 10 MMBF annually. Consequently, average annual lumber production per mill decreased from 13.5 MMBF in 1998 to 7.5 MMBF in 2002, and 6.9 MMBF for 2007 (table A14).

Table A13: Arizona sawmills by production size class, selected years (sources: Setzer and Wilson 1970; WWPA 1992, 1993; Keegan and others 2001a; Morgan and others 2006).

Year	Under 10 MMBF[a]	Over 10 MMBF[a]	Total
------------------Number of sawmills------------------			
2007	8	c	8
2002	9	2	11
1998	2	4	6
1990	5	9	14
1966	13	10	23
---Percentage of lumber output---			Volume (MBF[b])
2007	100	c	54,860
2002	25	75	82,658
1998	1	99	80,970
1990	4	96	388,000
1966	11	89	437,000

[a]Size class is based on reported lumber production. MMBF denotes million board feet lumber tally.

[b]MBF = thousand board feet lumber tally.

[c]All mills were included in <10 MMBF to avoid disclosing individual operations.

Table A14: Number of Arizona sawmills and average lumber production, selected years (sources: McLain 1988; Setzer and Wilson 1970; Keegan and others 2001a; Morgan and others 2006).

Year	Number of sawmills	Average lumber production
		MMBF[a]
2007	8	6.9
2002	11	7.5
1998	6	13.5
1990	14	27.7
1984	20	19.2
1966	23	19.0
1962	28	11.6
1960	38	8.7

[a]MMBF = million board feet lumber tally.

The State's four largest sawmills in 2007 produced an average of 12.7 MMBF, accounting for 93 percent of the lumber production, while the remaining four mills had an average lumber production of less than 1 MMBF (table A15).

On average, Arizona sawmills produced approximately 1.12 board feet of lumber for every board foot Scribner of timber processed for an average overrun of 12 percent in 2007. Overrun was 27 percent in 2002 (Morgan and others 2006) and 46 percent in 1998 (Keegan and others 2001a). The overrun decline was likely due to the dramatic shift of timber processed and the resulting size, condition, and product mix that could be recovered from the harvested timber. In 1998, about 64 percent of the lumber produced by Arizona's sawmills was dimension and studs, 35 percent was board and shop lumber, and less than one percent was timbers (Keegan and others 2001a). In 2002, only 22 percent of the lumber

USDA Forest Service Resour. Bull. RMRS-RB-13. 2012

17

Table A15: Arizona lumber production by mill size, 2007.

Size class[a]	Number of mills	Volume	Percentage of total	Average per mill
		MBF[b]		*MBF*[b]
Over 5 MMBF	4	50,890	93	12,723
Under 5 MMBF	4	3,970	7	993
Total	8	54,860	100	6,858

[a]Size class is based on reported lumber production. MMBF denotes million board feet lumber tally.

[b]MBF = thousand board feet lumber tally.

produced by Arizona's sawmills was dimension and studs; while 69 percent was board and shop lumber, and timbers, cants, or pallet stock constituted 19 percent of production (Morgan and others 2006). For 2007, only 4 percent of the lumber produced by Arizona's sawmills was dimension and studs; while 3 percent was board and shop lumber, and timbers, cants, or pallet stock constituted 93 percent of production.

Historically, the sawmill sector has accounted for more than 99 percent of wood products sales in Arizona. By 2002 that proportion had slipped to 79 percent, as timber harvest levels declined and the number of sawmills decreased. Sales from sawmills accounted for just 56 percent ($20.5 million) of finished products sales in 2007, decreasing from $27.7 million in 2002 (Morgan and others 2006). Of the sawmill products mine timbers, cants, and pallet stock accounted for $18.8 million (91.8 percent), board and shop lumber accounted for just under $1 million (4.5 percent) of sawmill sales in 2007, and dimension lumber was $ .76 million (3.7 percent) of sales. This was quite a shift in product balance from historical sales.

Log home Sector

Arizona's log home sector remained relatively unchanged from 2002. The number of house log manufacturers did not change from 2002 to 2007 (table A11). Only firms that process timber and manufacture house logs or log homes, not log home distributors, were included in the 1990, 1998, 2002 and 2007 censuses. In 2007, Arizona's five log home manufacturers processed 452 MBF Scribner of timber, produced about 139 MLF of house logs, and generated about $1.8 million in product sales. 2002 sales were higher by10 percent ($2 million), and both the volume of timber processed and volume of house logs produced decreased 8 and 17 percent respectively for 2007.

Other Products Sector

As with the sawmill sector fewer Arizona mills produced other primary wood products, with three less facilities operating in 2007 than in 2002 (table A11). Finished products sales by manufacturers of posts, poles, vigas, latillas, fuel pellets, and log furniture exceeded $14 million in 2007. A specific sales value was not reported in 2002 to avoid disclosure of firm level data (Morgan and others 2006); however, sales from the sector were estimated to have increased more than 180 percent from 2002 to 2007. Additional detail about the sector must be withheld to protect the confidentiality of firm level information.

Capacity and Utilization

Two aspects of capacity were examined for calendar year 2007 in Arizona and the other Four Corners States: production capacity and timber-processing capacity. Production capacity is defined as the amount of finished product that could be produced given sufficient supplies of raw materials and firm market demand for the products, considering normal maintenance and down time. Primary wood products producers specified annual and 8-hour shift production capacities in units of output (for example, MBF of lumber, MLF of house logs, number of vigas, etc.) for each firm. Product recovery ratios were calculated for each firm using reported timber input and product output volumes. Timber-processing capacity was defined as the volume of timber reported in MBF Scribner that could be processed given sufficient supplies of raw materials and firm market demand for the products, and was estimated for each firm by applying the product recovery ratios to production capacity.

Arizona's annual sawmill production capacity was 77,850 MBF of lumber in 2007. Producing 54,860 MBF of lumber, sawmills utilized about 70 percent of their lumber production capacity. Across all industry sectors, total timber-processing capacity was 84,857 MBF Scribner. Accounting for changes in log inventories, a total of 58,231 MBF Scribner was processed by Arizona firms in 2007, with timber-processing capacity utilization about 69 percent. Sawtimber-processing capacity was 141,480 MBF Scribner in 1998, with 53,458 MBF Scribner (38 percent) utilized (Keegan and others 2001a). In 2002, sawtimber-processing capacity fell to 98,025 MBF Scribner, with 71,260 MBF Scribner (73 percent) utilized. The decreased sawtimber-processing capacity and increased capacity utilization resulted from the permanent closure of two large sawmills, which were operating well below capacity in 1998.

Mill Residue Volumes, Types, and Uses

In 1998, Arizona's lone paper mill was the largest consumer of mill residues that were generated in the State. However, that mill shifted to using recycled material and did not use either roundwood pulpwood or mill residues in 2007. This change affected not only the ways and amounts of residues that were utilized, but it also impacted other sectors' ability to operate profitably. Sawmills, the leading timber processors, were also the main residue producers in Arizona. These facilities had to develop new markets for their residues, utilize the residues in-house, or consider cutting production to avoid generating more residue than could be disposed of affordably.

In 2007, Arizona mills produced 67,329 BDU, approximately 6,464 MCF of mill residue, with 98.5 percent utilized (table A16). Both residue production and the proportion utilized decreased from 1998. In 1998, Arizona sawmills generated 8,687 MCF, utilizing 99.9 percent (Keegan and others 2001a). Arizona's drop in residue utilization between 1998 and 2007 signaled a reversal of the long-term trend of increased residue utilization noted by Keegan and others (2001a) and was largely attributable to changes at the State's paper mill. The decrease in total residue volume generated, however, was attributable to sawmills processing less volume but creating more residues per unit of lumber produced because of the balance of products produced. In 1998, sawmills produced about 1.12 BDU per MBF of lumber; in 2007 that residue factor had increased to 1.22 BDU per MBF of lumber (table A17).

Table A16: Production and disposition of Arizona mill residues, 2007.

Residue type	Total utilized	Pulp and board	Energy	Mulch/ bedding	Unspecified use	Unused	Total produced
	---------------------------Bone-dry units[a]---------------------------						
Coarse	37,223	14,000	14,573	-	8,650	300	37,523
Fine	15,537	-	-	15,537	-	665	16,202
Sawdust	*8,676*	-	-	*8,676*	-	*640*	*9,316*
Planer shavings	*6,861*	-	-	*6,861*	-	*25*	*6,886*
Bark	13,536	-	2	5,814	7,720	68	13,604
Total	66,296	14,000	14,575	21,351	16,370	1,033	67,329
	---------------------------Percentage of residue type---------------------------						
Coarse	99.2	37.3	38.8	-	23.1	0.8	55.7
Fine	95.9	-	-	95.9	-	4.1	24.1
Sawdust	*93.1*	-	-	*93.1*	-	*6.9*	*13.8*
Planer shavings	*99.6*	-	-	*99.6*	-	*0.4*	*10.2*
Bark	99.5	-	0.0	42.7	56.7	0.5	20.2
Total	98.5	20.8	21.6	31.7	24.3	1.5	100

[a]Bone-dry unit = 2,400 lb oven-dry wood.

Table A17: Arizona sawmill residue factors, 1998, 2002 and 2007 (sources: Keegan and others 2001a; Morgan and others 2006).

Type of residue	1998	2002	2007
	------BDU/MBF lumber tally[a]--------		
Coarse	0.50	0.44	0.68
Sawdust	0.22	0.15	0.17
Planer shavings	0.19	0.14	0.12
Bark	0.21	0.23	0.25
Total	1.12	0.96	1.22

[a]Bone-dry unit (BDU = 2,400 lb oven-dry wood) of residue generated for every 1,000 board feet of lumber manufactured.

Three types of wood fiber residue have been produced by Arizona mills: coarse residue (chips) consisting of slabs, edging, trim, peelings, and log ends; fine residue consisting of planer shavings and sawdust; and bark. Coarse residue was the State's largest residue component at 37,523 BDUs (55.7 percent) of all residues in 2007, with 99 percent utilized. Out-of-State pulp and paper facilities used about 14,000 BDUs of the coarse material, with the remaining utilized volume going to energy and unspecified uses (table A16). Fine residues comprised the second largest component at 16,202 BDUs (24.1 percent) of mill residues. Only 95.9 percent of fine residue was utilized in 2007, primarily as mulch or animal bedding. Bark accounted for 20 percent of all residues and was largely used for mulch or unspecified products in 2007, with 13,536 BDU (99.5 percent) utilized.

Primary Forest Products Markets and Sales

Sales from Arizona's primary wood products industry in 2007 totaled $38.2 million, including finished products and mill residues (table A18). Lumber, mine

Table A18: Destination and sales value of Arizona's primary wood products and mill residues, 2007.

Product	Arizona	Other 4-Corner States	Other Rocky Mtn States[a]	Far West[b]	Northeast[c]	South[d]	North Central[e]	Other[f]	Total
				---Thousand 2007 dollars---					
Lumber, mine timbers, and other sawn products	$7,930	$9,557	$563	-	-	$1,584	$788	$90	$20,512
House logs and log homes	1,189	328	-	-	119	-	219	-	1,855
Other products[g]	5,307	8,092	-	2,440	-	-	-	-	15,839
Total	$14,426	$17,977	$563	$2,440	$119	$1,584	$1,007	$90	$38,206
				Percentage of regional sales by product					
Lumber, mine timbers, and other sawn products	55.0	53.2	100.0	-	-	100.0	78.3	-	53.7
House logs and log homes	8.2	1.8	-	-	-	-	21.7	-	4.9
Other products[g]	36.8	45.0	-	100.0	-	-	-	-	41.5
Total	37.8	47.1	1.5	6.4	0.3	4.1	2.6	0.2	100

[a]Other Rocky Mountains includes Idaho, Montana, Nevada.

[b]Far West includes Alaska, California, Hawaii, Oregon, and Washington.

[c]Northeast includes Connecticut, Maine, Massachusetts, New Hampshire, New Jersey, New York, Pennsylvania, Rhode Island, and Vermont.

[d]South includes Alabama, Arkansas, Delaware, Florida, Georgia, Kentucky, Louisiana, Maryland, Mississippi, North Carolina, Oklahoma, South Carolina, Tennessee, Texas, Virginia, and West Virginia.

[e]North Central includes Illinois, Indiana, Iowa, Kansas, Michigan, Minnesota, Missouri, Nebraska, North Dakota, Ohio, South Dakota, and Wisconsin.

[f]Other areas consist of products being shipped outside the United States.

[g]Other products include posts, poles, vigas, latillas, log furniture, mill residues, mulch, and fuel pellets.

timbers, and other sawn products accounted for 54 percent ($20.5 million) of total sales; house logs and log homes accounted for 5 percent ($1.9 million); while other products and mill residues accounted for 41 percent ($15.8 million). The other Four Corners States (Colorado, New Mexico, and Utah) were the leading markets for lumber, log homes, and other products which accounted for 47 percent of total sales. Arizona was second with in-State sales accounting for 37.8 percent of total sales, lumber playing a significant role. The Far West States were a major market area for other products, including mill residues.

Colorado

This chapter focuses on Colorado's timber harvest and forest products industry during 2007. Details of timber harvest, flow, and use are followed by descriptions of the primary processing sectors, capacity and utilization statistics, and mill residue characteristics. The chapter concludes with information on primary wood products industry sales by Colorado mills. Comparisons with previous years are provided where possible. Limited historical information is available about timber harvesting and mill production and residues in Colorado. The last comprehensive report on the State's industrial roundwood production and mill residues was conducted in 2002 (Morgan and others 2006) and data for previous years include 1962 (Spencer and Farrenkopf 1964), 1969 (Setzer 1971b), 1974 (Setzer and Shupe 1977), and 1982 (McLain 1985). More recently, Lynch and Mackes (2001)

USDA Forest Service Resour. Bull. RMRS-RB-13. 2012

21

provided a brief discussion of Colorado timber harvest in their study of wood use in Colorado from 1997 to 2000.

Timber Harvest, Flow, and Use

In 2008, Colorado had approximately 11.4 million acres of nonreserved timberland (Forest Inventory and Analysis 2009), with National Forests accounting for 69 percent, private owners accounting for 22 percent, and other public agencies accounting for the remaining 10 percent (table C1). All private timberland was classified as NIPF timberland. Colorado had no large tracts of timberland owned by entities operating primary wood processing facilities. Standing sawtimber volume on timberland was estimated at 16.3 billion cubic feet or approximately 85.8 billion board feet Scribner in 2008 (U.S. Department of Agriculture, FIDO 2009).

Timber Harvest

Colorado's 2007 commercial timber harvest was 86.5 MMBF Scribner, an 8.5 percent increase over 2002's harvest of 79.7 MMBF Scribner. The 2007 harvest was 21 percent less than the 1999 harvest of 110 MMBF reported by Lynch and Mackes (2001) and nearly 16 percent less than the 1982 harvest of 103 MMBF Scribner (McLain 1985). Only modest increases in Colorado's total annual timber harvest occurred despite increased salvage of dead timber, accounting for 55 percent (47.8 MMBF) of the 2007 harvest volume, more than doubling the 26 percent (20 MMBF) harvest of dead timber in 2002 (Morgan and others 2006). In 1982 dead trees accounted for just 8 percent of the total harvest volume (McLain 1985).

As in most of the Western States, decreasing Federal timber harvests have led to smaller total harvest volumes and greater shares of annual timber harvest coming from other ownership sources. However the National Forest's share of Colorado's timber harvest in 2007 was almost 50 percent. While in recent years private and tribal landowners provided the majority of Colorado's timber harvest, for 2007 they were down slightly at 48 percent. Lynch and Mackes (2001) indicated that National Forests provided about 47 percent of the 1999 harvest. In 2002, the National Forest's share of Colorado's timber harvest had dropped to 38 percent (table C2). In 1974 and 1982, National Forests accounted for 90 and 80 percent, respectively, of harvested volume (Setzer and Shupe 1977, McLain 1985). National Forests did provide the majority (78.5 percent) of house logs and other products harvested in 2007, but NIPF landowners provided the majority of sawlogs, and post and poles (table C3). Sawlogs accounted for about 84 percent (73 MMBF) of the total volume harvested, house logs and other products accounted for about 5 and 7 percent respectively, and posts and poles were about 3 percent of the harvest in 2007.

Table C1: Colorado nonreserved timberland by ownership class (source: Forest Inventory and Analysis program, 2008).

Ownership class	Thousand acres	Percentage of nonreserved timberland
National Forest	7,824	69
Private	2,456	22
Other public	1,117	10
Total	11,397	100

Table C2: Colorado timber harvest by ownership class, 1982, 2002 and 2007 (source: McLain 1985; Morgan and others 2006).

Ownership class	1982 MBF Scribner	1982 Percentage of total	2002 MBF Scribner	2002 Percentage of total	2007 MBF Scribner	2007 Percentage of total
Private and tr bal timberland	14,814	14.3	45,723	57.4	41,334	47.8
Private	*14,814*	*14.3*	*45,223*	*56.7*	*40,810*	*47.2*
Tribal	-	*0.0*	*500*	*0.6*	*524*	*0.6*
Public timberland	88,618	85.7	33,989	42.6	45,206	52.2
National Forest	*83,106*	*80.3*	*30,631*	*38.4*	*43,179*	*49.9*
State lands	*4,977*	*4.8*	*2,749*	*3.4*	*1,837*	*2.1*
Other public	*535*	*0.5*	*609*	*0.8*	*190*	*0.2*
All owners	103,448	100	79,711	100	86,540	100

Table C3: Colorado timber products harvested by ownership class, 2007.

Ownership class	Sawlogs	Post & pole	House logs	Other products[a]	All products
	-------Thousand board feet, Scribner--------				
National Forest	34,610	1,295	3,621	3,653	43,179
Private timberland	35,939	1,473	931	2,467	40,810
Other public lands	1,957	-	38	32	2,027
Tribal timberland	500	-	24	-	524
All owners	73,006	2,768	4,614	6,152	86,540
	-----Percentage of harvested product by ownership----				
National Forest	47.4	46.8	78.5	59.4	49.9
Private timberland	49.2	53.2	20.2	40.1	47.2
Other public lands	2.7	-	0.8	0.5	2.3
Tribal timberland	0.7	-	0.5	-	0.6
All owners	84.4	3.2	5.3	7.1	100

[a]Other products include furniture logs, fiber logs, viga logs, and logs delivered to primary manufacturers that became firewood.

During 2007, Grand County led Colorado's timber harvest with just over 35 percent (30.4 MMBF Scribner) of the volume; Delta and Mesa Counties followed with 15 and 6 percent, respectively (table C4). For the 2002 harvest, Garfield County led Colorado's timber harvest with just under 12 percent (9.3 MMBF Scribner) and Mesa and Las Animas Counties followed with 11 and 9 percent. In 1982, Jackson and Montezuma Counties led the harvest with more than 15 MMBF (14 percent) of the harvest each (McLain 1988).

Lodgepole pine was the leading species harvested in Colorado, accounting for 52 percent of the harvested volume in 2007 (table C5). This major shift in species harvested from past years mainly stemmed from massive numbers of lodgepole pine trees either killed by or threatened by mountain pine beetle attack. Aspen and cottonwood accounted for 20 percent, spruces, including Engelmann and blue spruce, accounted for almost 12 percent, while ponderosa pine accounted for 8 percent. Ponderosa pine was the most frequently harvested species by volume in 2002 (28 percent), followed by spruces at 25 percent, then aspen/cottonwood 19 percent and lodgepole pine at only 15 percent (Morgan and others 2006). In 1982, spruces were the leading species harvested, accounting for slightly more than 40 percent,

County	1974	1982	2002	2007	1974	1982	2002	2007
	------MBF Scribner-------				--Percentage of harvest--			
Adams	-	-	8	2	-	-	a	a
Alamosa	397	800	-	-	0.2	0.8	-	-
Archuleta	24,856	300	1,640	260	11.6	0.3	2.1	0.3
Boulder	90	514	44	3	a	0.5	0.1	a
Chaffee	-	252	595	48	-	0.2	0.7	0.1
Clear Creek	-	500	-	-	-	0.5	-	-
Conejos	6,007	1,221	740	618	2.8	1.2	0.9	0.7
Costilla	-	-	3,684	4,986	-	-	4.6	5.8
Custer	2,383	2,526	300	717	1.1	2.4	0.4	0.8
Delta	1,324	933	2,376	13,195	0.6	0.9	3.0	15.2
Dolores	12,687	7,801	5,907	3,275	5.9	7.5	7.4	3.8
Douglas	213	1,600	40	417	0.1	1.5	0.1	0.5
Eagle	5,221	1,500	200	-	2.4	1.5	0.3	-
Elbert	265	-	-	-	0.1	-	-	-
El Paso	285	470	240	49	0.1	0.5	0.3	0.1
Fremont	-	1,100	1,673	348	-	1.1	2.1	0.4
Garfield	2,218	500	9,321	1,924	1.0	0.5	11.7	2.2
Gilpin	-	-	20	-	-	-	a	-
Grand	18,406	618	3,113	30,387	8.6	0.6	3.9	35.1
Gunnison	12,431	2,336	4,249	4,110	5.8	2.3	5.3	4.7
Huerfano	2,192	1,800	500	500	1.0	1.7	0.6	0.6
Jackson	20,786	16,273	4,373	2,916	9.7	15.7	5.5	3.4
Jefferson	-	1,881	361	21	-	1.8	0.5	a
La Plata	39,950	1,271	2,312	321	18.7	1.2	2.9	0.4
Lake	-	-	844	-	-	-	1.1	-
Larimer	5,219	2,497	3,145	528	2.4	2.4	3.9	0.6
Las Animas	993	1,600	7,057	2,300	0.5	1.5	8.9	2.7
Logan	33	-	-	-	a	-	-	-
Mesa	5,252	1,765	8,660	4,973	2.5	1.7	10.9	5.7
Mineral	11,876	6,531	372	683	5.5	6.3	0.5	0.8
Moffat	158	-	124	-	0.1	-	0.2	-
Montezuma	4,169	15,001	4,495	3,242	1.9	14.5	5.6	3.7
Montrose	2,714	7,735	3,029	1,625	1.3	7.5	3.8	1.9
Ouray	-	2,565	30	8	-	2.5	a	a
Park	252	2,456	4,369	2,432	0.1	2.4	5.5	2.8
Pitkin	331	-	-	-	0.2	-	-	-
Pueblo	176	-	306	48	0.1	-	0.4	0.1
Rio Blanco	370	10	730	-	0.2	a	0.9	-
Rio Grande	10,857	9,277	557	100	5.1	9.0	0.7	0.1
Routt	10,442	1,976	1,143	2,008	4.9	1.9	1.4	2.3
Saguache	11,426	4,802	520	1,459	5.3	4.6	0.7	1.7
San Juan	-	-	274	-	-	-	0.3	-
San Miguel	-	2,131	1,020	-	-	2.1	1.3	-
Summit	-	193	289	2,606	-	0.2	0.4	3.0
Teller	46	713	1,049	432	a	0.7	1.3	0.5
Total	214,025	103,448	79,711	86,540	100	100	100	100

Table C4: Colorado timber harvest by county, selected years (sources: Setzer and Shupe 1977; McLain 1985; Morgan and others 2006).

aLess than 0.05 percent.

Table C5: Colorado timber harvest by species, selected years (sources: Setzer and Shupe 1977; McLain 1985; Morgan and others 2006).

Species	1974	1982	2002	2007	1974	1982	2002	2007
	------- MBF Scribner -------				---- Percentage of harvest ----			
Lodgepole pine	42,187	15,500	12,457	45,026	19.7	15.0	15.6	52.0
Aspen	4,825	12,737	15,292	17,319	2.3	12.3	19.2	20.0
Spruce[a]	91,638	41,877	19,908	10,203	42.8	40.5	25.0	11.8
Ponderosa pine	34,306	22,716	22,526	6,899	16.0	22.0	28.3	8.0
Douglas-fir	26,927	6,574	6,959	3,946	12.6	6.4	8.7	4.6
True firs[b]	14,142	3,986	2,512	3,132	6.6	3.9	3.2	3.6
Other species[c]	-	58	58	14	-	0.1	0.1	0.0
All species	214,025	103,448	79,711	86,539	100	100	100	100

[a]Spruce includes Engelmann and blue spruce.

[b]True firs include white and subalpine fir.

[c]Other species includegambel oak and western redcedar.

Table C6: Colorado timber harvest by species and product, 2007.

Species	Sawlogs	House logs	Posts and poles	Other products[a]	All products
	--------Thousand board feet, Scribner---------				
Lodgepole pine	42,187	1,277	1,317	246	45,026
Aspen	11,535	65	5	5,715	17,319
Spruce[b]	7,025	3,090	82	5	10,203
Ponderosa pine	5,667	41	1,019	171	6,899
Douglas-fir	3,472	136	335	2	3,946
True firs[c]	3,118	4	10	-	3,133
Other species[d]	2	-	-	12	14
All species	73,006	4,614	2,769	6,152	86,540
	------Percentage of product by species-------				
Lodgepole pine	57.8	28.5	8.9	4.0	52.0
Aspen	15.8	0.1	206.4	92.9	20.0
Spruce[b]	9.6	1.8	0.2	0.1	11.8
Ponderosa pine	7.8	22.1	6.2	2.8	8.0
Douglas-fir	4.8	7.3	0.1	0.0	4.6
True firs[c]	4.3	0.2	-	-	3.6
Other species[d]	0.0	-	0.4	0.2	0.0
All species	84.4	5.3	3.2	7.1	100

[a]Other products include furniture logs, fiber logs, viga logs, and logs delivered to primary manufacturers that became firewood.

[b]Spruce includes Engelmann and blue spruce.

[c]True firs include white and subalpine fir.

[d]Other species include gambel oak and western redcedar.

while ponderosa pine accounted for 22 percent (McLain 1985). Lodgepole pine and aspen were the leading species harvested for sawlogs in 2007, accounting for almost 58 and 16 percent, respectively (table C6). Spruces comprised 67 percent of the house log harvest, lodgepole pine was the leading species harvested for posts and poles, and aspen and cottonwood accounted for 93 percent of other products volume harvested.

Timber Flow

The majority (98 percent) of Colorado's 2007 timber harvest was processed in-State; during 2007 Colorado was a net importer of about 7.3 MMBF of timber. About 1.6 MMBF were exported for processing in Utah, and New Mexico; while 8.9 MMBF were imported from Utah, New Mexico, Wyoming, Arizona, Montana, Oklahoma, and Canada for processing in Colorado (table C7).

Timber processors in Colorado received 93,871 MBF of timber in 2007, including 8,968 MBF that was harvested outside the State. Private and tribal timberlands provided 48 percent of the timber delivered to Colorado mills in 2007, with 44,325 MBF coming from private lands and 534 MBF from tribal lands (table C8). National Forests provided about 46.6 percent (43,790MBF) of timber receipts, with 27—less than half—of Colorado's timber processors receiving timber cut from National Forests. During 2007, National Forests provided Colorado log home manufacturers with 84 percent of the house log volume processed in-State, NIPF landowners provided 14 percent, and less than 1 percent came from Canada. Private timberlands supplied the majority of sawlogs and posts and poles processed in Colorado, while public timberlands provided the majority of timber for other products.

Timber Use

Colorado's 2007 timber harvest—approximately 21,578 MCF, exclusive of bark (fig. C1)—was used by several manufacturing sectors both within and outside of Colorado. Of this volume, 13,362 MCF went as logs to sawmills, 918 MCF went to log home manufacturers, and 7,298 MCF went to post, pole, viga, latilla, log furniture, and excelsior manufacturers.

The following conversion factors were used to convert Scribner board foot volume to cubic feet:

- 5.08 board feet per cubic foot for house logs;
- 5.27 board feet per cubic foot for sawlogs;
- 2.21 board foot per cubic foot for all other products.

Of the 13,362 MCF of timber received by sawmills, 5,027 MCF (38 percent) was processed into finished lumber or other sawn products, and about 150 MCF was lost to shrinkage. The remaining 8,185 MCF (61 percent) yielded mill residue. About 8,076 MCF of sawmill residue was utilized, and about 123 MCF (1 percent) remained unused. Of the 918 MCF of timber received by log home manufacturers, about 603 MCF (66 percent) was manufactured into house logs, while the remaining 315 MCF became mill residue. About 305 MCF of house log residue was utilized, and about 10 MCF remained unused. Of the 7,298 MCF of timber

Table C7: Colorado timber products imports and exports, 2007.

Timber product	Imports	Exports	Net imports (net exports)
	--Thousand board feet, Scribner--		
Sawlogs	2,103	-	2,103
House logs	1,738	120	1,618
Other products[a]	5,127	1,517	3,610
All products	8,968	1,637	7,331

[a]Other products include furniture logs, fiber logs, viga logs, and logs delivered to primary manufacturers that became firewood.

Table C8: Timber received by Colorado forest products industry by ownership class and product, 2007.

Ownership class	Sawlogs	Posts and poles	House logs	Other products[a]	All products
			------Thousand board feet, Scribner--------		
Private and tr bal timberland	38,192	1,084	927	4,657	44,859
Private	37,692	1,084	893	4,657	44,325
Tribal	500	-	34	-	534
Public timberland	36,917	280	5,275	6,510	48,982
National Forest	34,610	280	5,237	3,663	43,790
State lands	2,157	-	13	2,832	5,002
Other public	150	-	25	15	190
Other owners	-	-	30	-	30
Other mills	-	-	-	-	-
Canada	-	-	30	-	30
All owners	75,109	1,364	6,232	11,167	93,871
			--------Percentage of product by owner--------		
Private and tr bal timberland	50.8	79.5	14.9	41.7	47.8
Private	50.2	79.5	14.3	41.7	47.2
Tribal	0.7	-	0.5	-	0.6
Public timberland	49.2	20.5	84.7	58.3	52.2
National Forest	46.1	20.5	84.0	32.8	46.6
State lands	2.9	-	0.2	25.4	5.3
Other public	0.2	-	0.4	0.1	0.2
Other owners	-	-	0.5	-	0.0
Other mills	-	-	-	-	-
Canada	-	-	0.5	-	0.0
All owners	80.0	1.5	6.6	11.9	100

[a]Other products include furniture logs, fiber logs, viga logs, and logs delivered to primary manufacturers that became firewood.

received by other manufacturers, nearly 6,409 MCF was utilized in solid wood products (such as posts, poles, vigas, latillas, and log furniture) or was used in the production of excelsior. About 885 MCF of residues from these other sectors were utilized and 4 MCF went unused.

Forest Industry Sectors

Colorado's primary forest products industry in 2007 consisted of 64 active manufacturers in 28 counties (table C9). Facilities tended to be located near the forest resource in the central and southwestern portions of the State (fig. C2). The sawmill sector, manufacturing lumber and other sawn products, was the largest sector operating in 2007 with 30 mills; 19 facilities produced house logs and log homes. There were nine log furniture producers, five post and pole firms, and an excelsior producer also operating in 2007. Morgan and others (2006) identified 133 primary wood-processing plants in 2002: 50 sawmills, 46 house log plants, 10 post and pole facilities, and 27 facilities producing log furniture and other products including a shake mill, and an excelsior manufacturer. Changes in Colorado's industry structure over the past 20 years were similar to those experienced throughout the West, with the number of sawmills decreasing and the number and diversity of

USDA Forest Service Resour. Bull. RMRS-RB-13. 2012

27

Colorado Timber Harvest and Flow, 2007

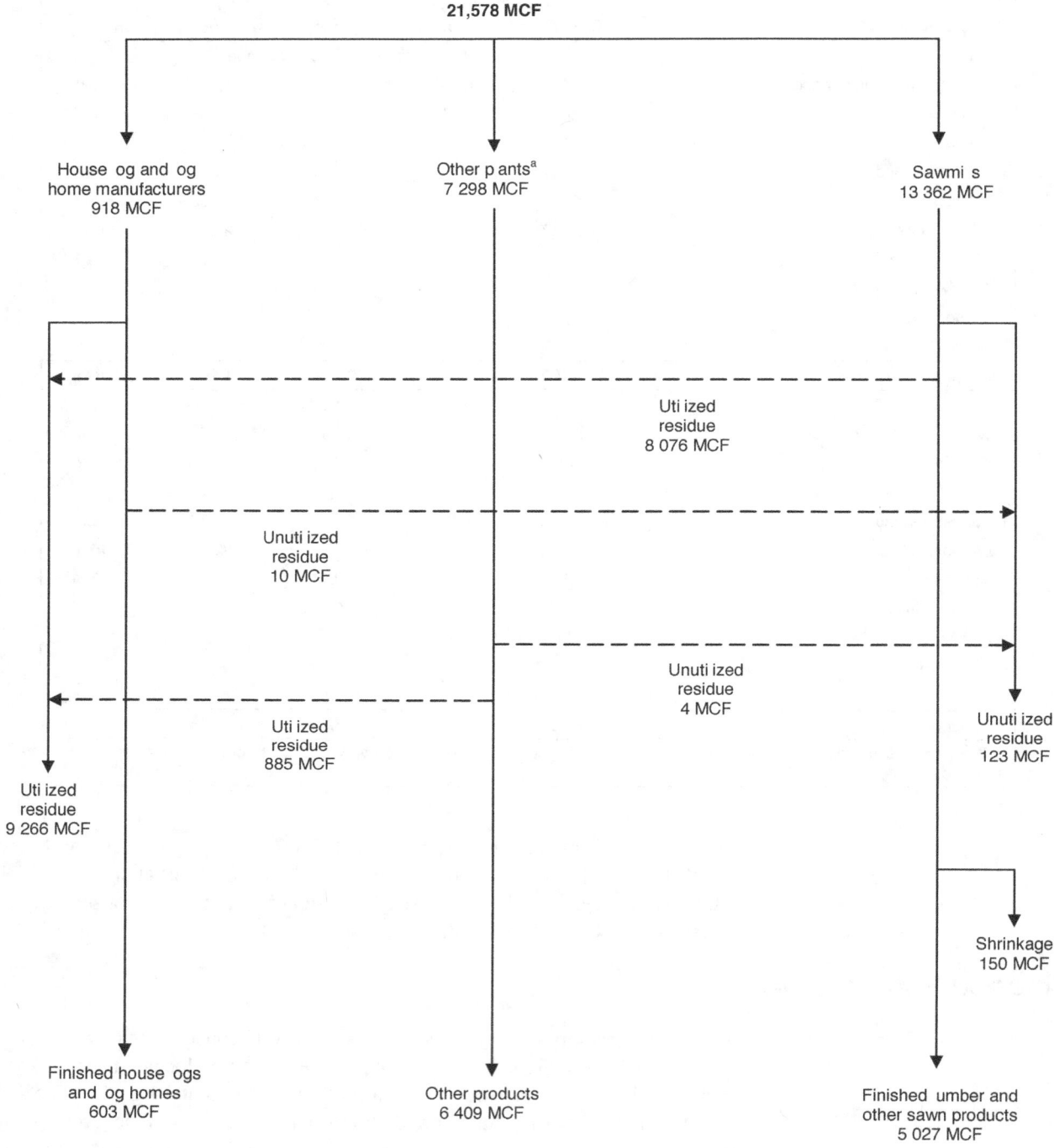

Total Harvest
21,578 MCF

House ogs and og
home manufacturers
918 MCF

Other p ants[a]
7 298 MCF

Sawmi s
13 362 MCF

Uti ized
residue
8 076 MCF

Unuti ized
residue
10 MCF

Unuti ized
residue
4 MCF

Uti ized
residue
885 MCF

Unuti ized
residue
123 MCF

Uti ized
residue
9 266 MCF

Shrinkage
150 MCF

Finished house ogs
and og homes
603 MCF

Other products
6 409 MCF

Finished umber and
other sawn products
5 027 MCF

Figure C1: Colorado timber harvest and flow, 2007.

Table C9: Active Colorado primary wood products facilities by county and product, 2007 (sources: McLain 1985; Morgan and others 2006).

County	Lumber	Log homes and house logs	Post and pole	Log furniture and other products[a]	Total
Arapahoe				1	1
Archuleta	3				3
Boulder	1			1	2
Conejos	2				2
Custer	1				1
Delta	3				3
Denver				1	1
Eagle	1				1
El Paso				1	1
Fremont	2		1		3
Garfield	2	1			3
Grand	1	1	2	1	5
Huerfano	1				1
Jefferson				1	1
La Plata	1	3			4
Larimer	3	1	1	1	6
Las Animas	1				1
Mesa	1				1
Mineral		1			1
Montezuma	3		1	1	5
Montrose	2	4		1	7
Park		3			3
Rio Grande	1				1
Routt		2			2
Saguache		1			1
Summit		1		1	2
Teller	1				1
Weld		1			1
2007 Total	**30**	**19**	**5**	**10**	**64**
2002 Total	50	46	10	27	133
1982 Total	84	5	4	2	95

[a]Other products include excelsior.

other manufacturers increasing (Keegan and others 2001a,b; Morgan and others 2004 a,b; Morgan and others 2006).

Historic sales values for Colorado's primary wood products producers were not provided by Setzer (1971b), Setzer and Shupe (1977), or McLain (1985). In 2007, sales value of finished products from Colorado's primary wood products industry totaled $101 million. This compares to 2002 sales of $109 million in 2007 dollars (table C10). Sales from sawmills accounted for 44 percent, about the same as 2002; house log and log home manufacturers accounted for 24 percent, a 5 percent drop from 2002; and other products manufacturers accounted for about 33 percent, an increase from 2002 of about 5 percent of finished products sales.

USDA Forest Service Resour. Bull. RMRS-RB-13. 2012

29

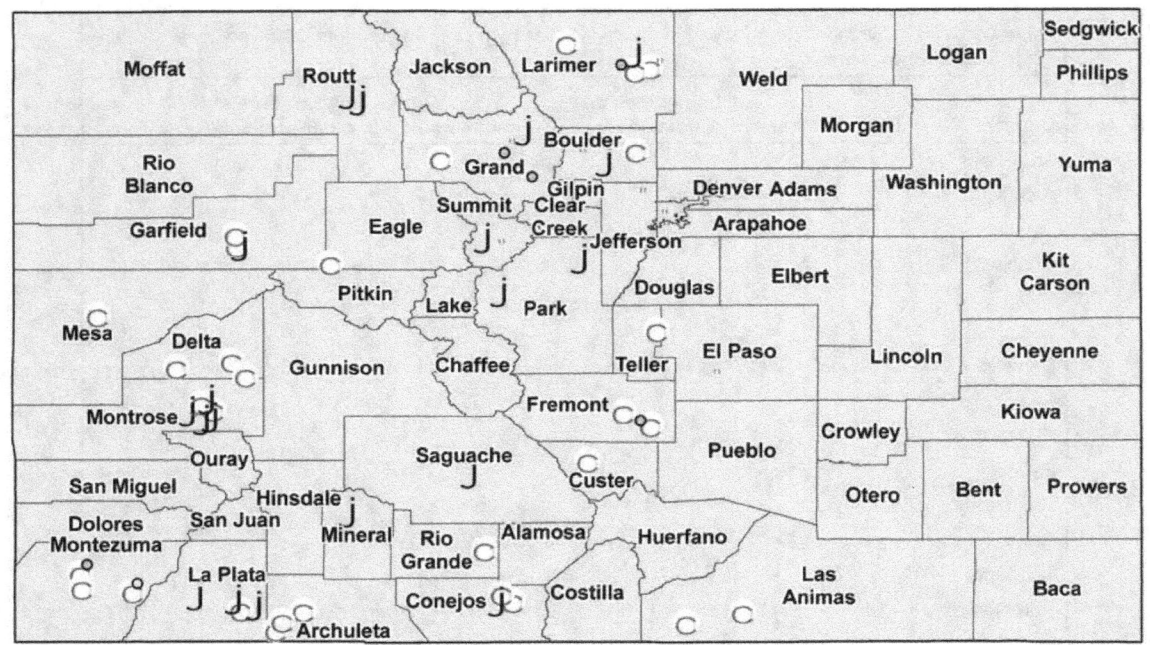

Colorado facilities

j   House Log/ Log Home

    Log Furniture

o   Other

⊙   Post/ Pole/ Piling

C   Sawmill

Figure C2: Map of Colorado facilities.

Table C10: Finished product sales of Colorado's primary wood products sectors, 2007 (source: Morgan and others 2006).		
Sector	**2002**	**2007**
	--------*Thousands of 2007 dollars*[a]--------	
Sawmills	$47,193	$45,043
Log homes	31,808	19,460
Other sectors[b]	30,136	36,652
Total	$109,137	$101,155
[a]All sales are reported f.o.b. the manufacturer's plant.		
[b]Other sectors include producers of posts, poles, log furniture, and excelsior.		

Sawmill Sector

The number of sawmills in Colorado decreased from 84 in 1982 (McLain 1985) to 50 in 2002 and to 30 in 2007 (table C11), with 20 sawmills closing between 2002 and 2007. Total lumber production in the State increased 39 percent from about 83 MMBF in 2002 (Morgan and others 2006) to115 MMBF, the average production per mill increased 129 percent from 1.7 MMBF to 3.9 MMBF. This increase is a function of fewer mills producing more volume. The State's nine largest sawmills in 2007 produced an average of 11,788 MBF, and seven of these mills produced between 2,000 MBF and 5,000 MBF. The remaining 21 mills produced less than 442 MBF of lumber (table C12).

Technological improvements have made Colorado mills more efficient. For example, thinner kerf saws reduce the proportion of the log that becomes sawdust. Additionally, mill-delivered log diameters are believed to have decreased over the past 25 years, with reduced old-growth harvesting and increased use of restoration and fuels treatments that favor retention of larger trees and the removal of smaller stems. As log diameters decrease, the Scribner log rule, which is used in Colorado, under estimates—by an increasing amount—the volume of lumber that can be recovered from a log, thus increasing overrun. On average, Colorado sawmills produced approximately 1.54 board feet of lumber for every board foot Scribner of timber processed for an average overrun of 54 percent in 2007, slightly higher than the 47 percent overrun in 2002 (Morgan and others 2006). Overrun was estimated to be 17 percent in 1982, using WWPA's (1983) lumber production and McLain's (1985) sawlog consumption. This overrun increase was attributed to improved milling technology and the increased use of smaller diameter timber.

Table C11: Number of Colorado sawmills and average lumber production, selected years (source: McLain 1985; WWPA 1983; Morgan and others 2006).

Year	Number of sawmills	Average lumber production
		MMBF[a]
2007	31	3.8
2002	50	1.7
1982	84	1.4[b]

[a]MMBF = million board feet lumber tally.

[b]Total production 118 MMBF.

Table C12: Colorado lumber production by mill size, 2007.

Size class[a]	Number of mills	Volume	Percentage of total	Average per mill
		MBF[b]		MBF[b]
Over 2 MMBF	10	108,289	93	10,829
Under 2 MMBF	21	7,843	7	373
Total	31	116,132	100	3,746

[a]Size class is based on reported lumber production. MMBF denotes million board feet lumber tally.

[b]MBF = thousand board feet lumber tally.

USDA Forest Service Resour. Bull. RMRS-RB-13. 2012

31

Sales from sawmills declined from 2002 to 2007, accounting for just 43.5 percent ($44 million) of Colorado timber processors' finished products sales in 2007; this parallels 2002 numbers of 43 percent ($41.5 million) (Morgan and others 2006). In comparison; sawmill sales accounted for 56 and 49 percent of timber processors' finished product sales in Arizona and New Mexico, respectively, during 2007, and historically accounted for 90 percent or more of sales throughout the Interior West (Keegan and others 2001a,b,c; Morgan and others 2004b). Dimension lumber and studs accounted for $28.1 million (64 percent) of sawmill product sales in 2007; other sawn products accounted for $7.3 million (17 percent); mine timbers, cants, and railroad ties accounted for $5 million (11 percent); board and shop lumber accounted for $2.2 million (5 percent); and other miscellaneous products accounted for nearly $1.4 million (3 percent) of finished product sales from sawmills.

Log Home Sector

Colorado's log home sector experienced substantial growth and then a decline over the past 25 years. Twenty-seven less facilities were identified in 2007 than in 2002, whereas 41 more house log manufacturers were identified in 2002 than in 1982 (table C9). Only firms that processed timber and manufactured house logs or log homes, not log home distributors, were included in the 1982, 2002 and 2007 censuses. In 2007, Colorado's 19 log home manufacturers processed almost 6 MMBF Scribner of timber, produced about 1.3 million lineal feet (MMLF) of house logs, and generated $19.5 million in product sales. By sales value, Colorado's log home industry is the third largest in the Western United States behind Montana and Idaho.

Other Products Sectors

Following the same trend as the log home sector, Colorado's producers of posts and poles and other primary wood products significantly expanded production from 1982 to 2002; production then declined from 2002 to 2007. There were 21 less manufacturers operating in this sector in 2007 compared to 2002, while 31 more facilities operated in 2002 than in 1982 (table C9). In 2007, nine of these other products facilities manufactured log furniture, five were post and pole producers, and one was an excelsior plant. Finished products sales by manufacturers of posts and poles exceeded $9 million, and sales by manufacturers of log furniture and excelsior exceeded $30 million in 2007. Additional detail about this sector is withheld to protect the confidentiality of firm level information.

Capacity and Utilization

Colorado's annual sawmill production capacity was 205.5 MMBF of lumber in 2007. Sawmills produced 115.4 MMBF of lumber in 2007, utilizing 56 percent of their lumber production capacity. This was an increase from the historically low level of 35 percent production capacity utilization of reported in 2002 (Morgan and others 2006). Timber-processing capacity among Colorado sawmills was 121,927 MBF Scribner, with 72,007 MBF Scribner of timber processed, making utilization of timber-processing capacity among sawmills about 59 percent in 2007. Across all industry sectors, total timber-processing capacity was 144,308 MBF Scribner. Accounting for changes in mills' log inventories, a total of 93,894 MBF Scribner was processed by Colorado firms in 2007, making timber-processing capacity utilization about 65 percent across all sectors. The greater timber-processing capacity utilization of all sectors compared to sawmills alone would indicate that processors other than sawmills were operating near their total timber capacity and are better positioned to utilize the mix of timber being offered in Colorado.

Mill Residue Volumes, Types, and Uses

Sawmills, the leading timber processors, were also the main residue producers in Colorado. In 2007, sawmills produced 1.04 BDU of residue per MBF of lumber (table C13). Across all sectors, Colorado timber processors produced 121,982 BDU, approximately 11,729 MCF of mill residue, with 98.7 percent utilized (table C14). Total residue production declined from 22,749 MCF in 1974 and 12,420 MCF in 1982, but increased from 9,115 MCF in 2002, while the proportion utilized increased from 40 percent in 1974 to 64 percent in 1982 (McLain 1985), to 98 percent in 2002 (Morgan and others 2006). Colorado's decreased residue production stemmed from increased milling efficiencies working in concert with decreased timber volumes processed. Increased residue utilization between 1974 and 2007 was attributable to decreased residue production and the evolution of better markets for residue-related products.

Coarse residue was the State's largest residue component at 57 percent (69,552 BDU) of all residues in 2007, with 99 percent utilized. Out-of-State pulp, paper, and reconstituted board facilities used 43,300 BDUs of the coarse material; the remaining volume was used for energy production and unspecified uses (table C14). Fine residues comprised the second largest component at 30 percent (36,639 BDUs) of mill residues. Almost 98 percent of fine residue was utilized in 2007, primarily for energy, with a little over one-third of fine residues going to mulch or animal bedding facilities. Bark accounted for 13 percent of all residues and was largely burned for energy or used for mulch in 2007, with 15,596 BDUs (98 percent) utilized.

Primary Forest Products Markets and Sales

Sales from Colorado's primary wood products industry during 2007 totaled nearly $104 million, including finished products and mill residues (table C15). Lumber, mine timbers, and other sawn products accounted for 43 percent (over $45 million) of total sales; house logs and log homes accounted for 19 percent (over $19 million); while other products and mill residues accounted for 29 percent (slightly over $30 million). Colorado was the leading market area for lumber, log homes, posts, poles, and log furniture, within-State sales accounting for 47 percent of total sales. The other Four Corners States (Arizona, New Mexico, and Utah)

Table C13: Colorado's sawmill residue factors, 2002 and 2007 (source: Morgan and others 2006).		
Type of residue	2002	2007
	----BDU/MBF lumber tally[a]---	
Coarse	0.42	0.60
Sawdust	0.17	0.21
Planer shavings	0.13	0.09
Bark	0.29	0.14
Total	1.01	1.04
[a]Bone-dry unit (BDU = 2,400 lb oven-dry wood) of residue generated for every 1,000 board feet of lumber manufactured.		

Table C14: Production and disposition of Colorado mill residues, 2007.

Residue type	Total utilized	Pulp and board	Energy	Mulch/ bedding	Unspecified use	Unused	Total produced
			---Bone-dry units[a]---				
Coarse	68,949	43,300	11,070	-	14,579	603	69,552
Fine	35,857	-	22,508	13,349	-	782	36,639
Sawdust	25,378	-	16,001	9,377	-	598	25,976
Planer shavings	10,479	-	6,507	3,972	-	184	10,663
Bark	15,596	-	9,916	5,564	116	195	15,791
Total	120,402	43,300	43,494	18,913	14,695	1,580	121,982
			---Percentage of residue type---				
Coarse	99.1	62.3	15.9	-	21.0	0.9	57.0
Fine	97.9	-	61.4	36.4	-	2.1	30.0
Sawdust	97.7	-	61.6	36.1	-	2.3	21.3
Planer shavings	98.3	-	61.0	37.3	-	1.7	8.7
Bark	98.8	-	62.8	35.2	0.7	1.2	12.9
Total	98.7	35.5	35.7	15.5	12.0	1.3	100

[a]Bone-dry unit = 2,400 lb oven-dry wood.

Table C15: Destination and sales value of Colorado's primary wood products and mill residues, 2007.

Product	Colorado	Other 4-Corner States	Other Rocky Mtn States[a]	Far West[b]	Northeast[c]	South[d]	North Central[e]	Other[f]	Total
				---Thousand 2007 dollars---					
Lumber, mine timbers and other sawn products	$32,874	$7,380	$1,905	$200	$28	$1,165	$1,490	-	$45,042
House logs and log homes	9,929	3,581	656	304	274	3,588	1,128	-	19,460
Posts, poles, and log furniture	3,742	1,825	679	529	697	1,045	625	-	9,142
Other products[g]	2,383	5,886	2,898	4,701	386	7,913	3,800	2,186	30,153
Total	$48,928	$18,672	$6,138	$5,734	$1,385	$13,711	$7,043	$2,186	$103,797
				---Percentage of product sales by region---					
Lumber, mine timbers and other sawn products	73.0	16.4	4.2	0.4	0.1	2.6	3.3	-	43.4
House logs and log homes	51.0	18.4	3.4	1.6	1.4	18.4	5.8	-	18.7
Posts, poles, and log furniture	40.9	20.0	7.4	5.8	7.6	11.4	6.8	-	8.8
Other products[g]	7.9	19.5	9.6	15.6	1.3	26.2	12.6	7.2	29.0
Total	47.1	18.0	5.9	5.5	1.3	13.2	6.8	2.1	100

[a]Other Rocky Mountains includes Idaho, Montana, Nevada.

[b]Far West includes Alaska, California, Hawaii, Oregon, and Washington.

[c]Northeast includes Connecticut, Maine, Massachusetts, New Hampshire, New Jersey, New York, Pennsylvania, Rhode Island, and Vermont.

[d]South includes Alabama, Arkansas, Delaware, Florida, Georgia, Kentucky, Louisiana, Maryland, Mississippi, North Carolina, Oklahoma, South Carolina, Tennessee, Texas, Virginia, and West Virginia.

[e]North Central includes Illinois, Indiana, Iowa, Kansas, Michigan, Minnesota, Missouri, Nebraska, North Dakota, Ohio, South Dakota, and Wisconsin.

[f]Other areas consist of products being shipped outside the U.S.

[g]Other products include excelsior, firewood, and mill residues.

accounted for about 18 percent of total sales; the majority of revenues were generated from sales of lumber and log home products. The Southern U.S. accounted for over 13 percent of total sales, 18 percent of log home sales and 26 percent of other products sales. The North Central States, Far West, and Northeast were major market areas for other products, including excelsior and mill residues.

This chapter focuses on New Mexico's timber harvest and forest products industry during 2007, and discusses changes that occurred since the 2002 industry census conducted by Morgan and others (2006). Details of timber harvest, flow, and use are followed by descriptions of the primary processing sectors, capacity and utilization statistics, and mill residue characteristics. This chapter concludes with information on New Mexico's primary wood products industry sales.

Timber Harvest, Flow, and Use

In 2003, New Mexico had approximately 4.4 million acres of nonreserved timberland (O'Brien 2003), with National Forests accounting for 64 percent, private and tribal owners accounting for 33 percent, and other public agencies accounting for the remaining 3 percent (table N1). All private timberland was classified as NIPF timberland. With the exception of several Native American tribes, New Mexico had no large tracts of timberland owned by entities operating primary wood processing facilities. Sawtimber volume on nonreserved timberlands was estimated at 5.1 billion cubic feet or approximately 29.1 billion board feet Scribner in 2008 (U.S. Department of Agriculture, FIDO 2009).

Timber Harvest

New Mexico's 2007 commercial timber harvest was 39,770 MBF Scribner, 53 percent of the 2002 harvest, and 40 percent of the 1997 harvest (Morgan and others 2006; Keegan and others 2001b). The reduction in New Mexico's total annual timber harvest since the late 1980s was primarily due to the decline of National Forest timber harvest. As National Forest and total timber harvest in the State declined, a disproportionate and diminishing share of New Mexico's timber harvest came from National Forest timberlands (table N2). In 1966, 1969, 1974, and 1986 National Forests accounted for 50 percent or more of harvested volume (Setzer and Wilson 1970; Setzer 1971c; Setzer and Barrett 1977; McLain 1989), whereas in 2002 and 2007 National Forests accounted for 14 percent of the harvest volume (Morgan and others 2006). Unlike other States in the region where National Forests provided the majority of house logs harvested, the majority of each of the timber products harvested in New Mexico came from private and tribal timberlands, and National Forests provided less than 20 percent of each product, except the other products category, which was almost 40 percent from National Forest (table N3). Sawlogs accounted for almost 83 percent (33 MMBF) of the total volume harvested.

Table N1: New Mexico nonreserved timberland by ownership class (source: O'Brien 2003).		
Ownership class	**Thousand acres**	**Percentage of nonreserved timberland**
National Forest	2,810	64
Private and tribal	1,448	33
Other public	146	3
Total	4,404	100

USDA Forest Service Resour. Bull. RMRS-RB-13. 2012

35

Table N2: New Mexico timber harvest by ownership class, 1997, 2002 and 2007 (source: Keegan and others 2001b; Morgan and others 2006).

Ownership class	1997 MBF Scribner	1997 Percentage of total	2002 MBF Scribner	2002 Percentage of total	2007 MBF Scribner	2007 Percentage of total
Private and tr bal timberland	85,903	88.0	64,201	86.3	33,001	83.0
Private	*61,853*	*63.4*	*36,821*	*49.5*	*14,971*	*37.6*
Tribal	*24,050*	*24.6*	*27,380*	*36.8*	*18,030*	*45.3*
Public timberland	11,723	12.0	10,160	13.7	6,769	17.0
National Forest	*11,723*	*12.0*	*10,160*	*13.7*	*5,644*	*14.2*
State timberland	-	-	-	-	*1,125*	*2.8*
All owners	97,626	100	74,361	100	39,770	100

Table N3: New Mexico timber products harvested by ownership class, 2007.

Ownership class	Sawlogs	Vigas	House logs	Other products[a]	All products
	--------Thousand of board feet, Scribner---------				
Tribal timberland	18,030	-	-	-	18,030
Private timberland	11,388	1,758	95	1,730	14,971
National Forest	3,409	435	-	1,800	5,644
State timberland	-	-	-	1,125	1,125
All owners	32,827	2,193	95	4,655	39,770
	-----Percentage of harvested product by ownership------				
Tribal timberland	54.9	-	-	-	45.3
Private timberland	34.7	80.2	100.0	37.2	37.6
National Forest	10.4	19.8	-	38.7	14.2
State timberland	-	-	-	24.2	2.8
All owners	82.5	5.5	0.2	11.7	100

[a]Other products include posts, poles, furniture logs, fiber logs, and logs delivered to primary manufacturers that became firewood.

In 2007, as in 2002, Otero County led New Mexico's timber harvest with slightly more than 47 percent of total volume; Colfax and Sandoval Counties followed, with 24 and 6 percent, respectively (table N4). Otero County has accounted for an increasing share of New Mexico's timber harvest, with 7 percent in 1966, 10 percent in 1986, 38 percent in 1997, and 42 percent in 2002. Historically, Rio Arriba has been among the State's top three timber-producing counties, accounting for 15 percent or more of annual harvest volumes until 2007 when it only contributed 4.4 percent. Colfax County, however, was not a significant contributor to New Mexico's annual harvest until 2007, only periodically accounting for more than 10 percent of harvest in previous censuses (Setzer and Wilson 1970; McLain 1989; Keegan and others 2001b; Morgan and others 2006).

Ponderosa pine continued to be the leading species harvested in New Mexico, accounting for nearly 47 percent of the harvest in 2007; Douglas-fir retained its long-held position as the second most harvested species (table N5). White and subalpine firs and Engelmann spruce together accounted for about 20 percent of the 2007 harvest. Ponderosa pine was the leading species harvested for sawlogs, vigas, and house logs in 2007 (table N6). Douglas-fir and true firs were substantial components of the sawlog harvest, while Engelmann spruce was a minor component

Table N4: New Mexico timber harvest by county, selected years (sources: Setzer and Wilson 1970; McLain 1989; Keegan and others 2001b; Morgan and others 2006).

County	1966	1986	1997	2002	2007	1966	1986	1997	2002	2007
	------------MBF Scribner------------					-------Percentage-------				
Bernalillo	691	-	490	100	-	0.3	-	0.5	0.1	-
Catron	25,588	29,494	2,973	250	1,500	10.6	17.7	3.0	0.3	3.8
C bola	-	13,857	7,973	15	-	-	8.3	8.2	a	-
Colfax	32,853	4,000	18,450	3,777	9,423	13.6	2.4	18.9	5.1	23.7
Eddy	-	548	-	-	-	-	0.3	-	-	-
Grant	538	663	-	-	279	0.2	0.4	-	-	0.7
Lincoln	-	1,450	198	-	1,800	-	0.9	0.2	-	4.5
Los Alamos	54	-	-	-	-	a	-	-	-	-
McKinley	36,692	-	2,000	-	-	15.1	-	2.0	-	-
Mora	957	3,830	2,040	10,864	215	0.4	2.3	2.1	14.6	0.5
Otero	17,335	16,982	36,866	30,825	18,835	7.2	10.2	37.8	41.5	47.4
Rio Arr ba	37,156	69,367	17,107	17,869	1,733	15.3	41.7	17.5	24.0	4.4
Sandoval	66,619	5,932	4,360	1,200	2,190	27.5	3.6	4.5	1.6	5.5
San Juan	-	8,159	500	-	-	-	4.9	0.5	-	-
San Miguel	9,140	2,075	2,259	8,100	795	3.8	1.2	2.3	10.9	2.0
Santa Fe	-	2,865	-	670	1,000	-	1.7	-	0.9	2.5
Socorro	2,739	-	1,025	220	-	1.1	-	1.0	0.3	-
Taos	6,767	7,066	1,245	175	2,000	2.8	4.2	1.3	0.2	5.0
Torrance	-	-	120	175	-	-	-	0.1	0.2	-
Valencia	4,548	-	20	120	-	1.9	-	a	0.2	-
Total[b]	242,313	166,342	97,626	74,361	39,770	100	100	100	100	100

[a]Less than 0.05 percent.

[b]Percentage detail may not sum to 100% due to rounding.

Table N5: New Mexico timber harvest by species, selected years (sources: Setzer and Wilson 1970; McLain 1989; Keegan and others 2001b; Morgan and others 2006).

Species	1966	1986	1997	2002	2007
	--------Percentage of harvest---------				
Ponderosa pine	49	68	57	50	47
Douglas-fir	17	16	26	22	25
True firs[a]	5	9	11	16	17
Other species[b]	15	4	<0.5	2	8
Engelmann spruce	14	3	7	10	3
All species	100	100	100	100	100

[a]True firs include white and subalpine fir.

[b]Other species include limber pine and aspen.

of house logs at 13 percent. Engelmann spruce and Douglas-fir were also small components of the viga harvest. Ponderosa pine was the leading species harvested for other products, while aspen and other species were also significant components to the other product category, which includes posts, poles, furniture logs, and fire wood logs.

USDA Forest Service Resour. Bull. RMRS-RB-13. 2012

37

Table N6: New Mexico timber harvest by species and product, 2007.

Species	Sawlogs	Vigas	House logs	Other products[a]	All products
	-------Thousand of board feet, Scribner-------				
Ponderosa pine	14,334	1,416	43	2,786	18,579
Douglas-fir	9,283	379	-	281	9,943
White fir	6,699	170	40	-	6,909
Lodgepole pine	1,444	-	-	113	1,557
Other species[b]	9	-	-	1,475	1,484
Engelmann spruce	1,058	228	12	-	1,298
All species	32,827	2,193	95	4,655	39,770
	--------Percentage of product by species-------				
Ponderosa pine	43.7	64.6	45.3	59.9	46.7
Douglas-fir	28.3	17.3	-	6.0	25.0
White fir	20.4	7.8	42.1	-	17.4
Lodgepole pine	4.4	-	-	2.4	3.9
Other species[b]	0.0	-	-	31.7	3.7
Engelmann spruce	3.2	10.4	12.6	-	3.3
All species	82.5	5.5	0.2	11.7	100

[a]Other products include posts, poles, furniture logs, fiber logs, and logs delivered to primary manufacturers that became firewood.

[b]Other species include alligator juniper, Rocky Mountain juniper, two-needle pinyon, Western redcedar, and Aspen.

Timber Flow

The vast majority (93 percent) of New Mexico's 2007 timber harvest was processed in State; however, New Mexico was a net exporter of timber. Almost 3 MMBF were exported for processing in Colorado, while a small amount of timber was imported from Colorado for processing in New Mexico (table N7).

Timber processors in New Mexico received 37,917 MBF of timber in 2007, including 1,125 MBF that was harvested outside the State. Timber receipts dropped nearly 45 percent since 2002, when New Mexico mills received 68,858 MBF of timber. Ownership sources of timber delivered to New Mexico mills changed slightly since 2002, with the proportion from private and tribal lands decreasing from 85 percent to 79 percent in 2007 (table N8). National Forests supplied timber to 10—less than a half—of New Mexico's mills in 2007, accounting for 18 percent of mill receipts, which was an increase from 2002 when National Forests supplied just 15 percent of the timber received by New Mexico mills. Unlike other States in the region, National Forests did not provide New Mexico forest products manufacturers with a large portion of timber products, supplying less than 11 percent of sawlogs, 26 percent of vigas, no house logs, but 60 percent of other products, mostly post and poles and firewood logs to the industry in 2007 (table N9).

Timber Use

New Mexico's 2007 timber harvest—approximately 10,813 MCF, exclusive of bark (fig. N1)—was used by several manufacturing sectors both within and outside of New Mexico. Of this volume, 5,673 MCF went as logs to sawmills, 485 MCF went to log home and viga manufacturers, and 4,655 MCF went to other plants,

Table N7: New Mexico timber products imports and exports, 2007.

Timber product	Imports	Exports	Net imports (net exports)
	-------Thousand board feet, Scribner-------		
Sawlogs	-	1,548	(1,548)
House logs	-	15	(15)
Other products[a]	1,125	1,415	(290)
All products	1,125	2,978	(1,853)

[a]Other products include posts, poles, furniture logs, fiber logs, and logs delivered to primary manufacturers that became firewood.

Table N8: Ownership of timber products received by New Mexico mills, 1997, 2002 and 2007 (sources: Keegan and others 2001b; Morgan and others 2006).

	1997		2002		2007	
Ownership class	MBF Scribner	Percentage of total	MBF Scribner	Percentage of total	MBF Scribner	Percentage of total
Private and tribal timberland	82,238	90.6	58,698	85.2	30,023	79.2
Private	57,788	63.6	31,318	45.5	11,993	31.6
Tribal	24,450	26.9	27,380	39.8	18,030	47.6
National Forests	8,562	9.4	10,160	14.8	6,769	17.9
State Lands	-	-	-	-	1,125	3.0
All owners	90,800	100	68,858	100	37,917	100

Table N9: Timber received by New Mexico forest products industry by ownership class and product, 2007.

Ownership class	Sawlogs	Vigas	House logs	Other products[a]	All products
	----------Thousand of board feet, Scribner----------				
Tribal timberland	18,030	-	-	-	18,030
Private timberland	9,840	1,258	80	815	11,993
National Forest	3,409	435	-	2,925	6,769
State lands	-	-	-	1,125	1,125
All owners	31,279	1,693	80	4,865	37,917
	-------Percentage of product by owner--------				
Tribal timberland	57.6	-	-	-	47.6
Private timberland	31.5	74.3	100.0	16.8	31.6
National Forest	10.9	25.7	-	60.1	17.8
State lands	-	-	-	23.1	3.0
All owners	82.5	4.5	0.2	12.8	100

[a]Other products include posts, poles, fiber logs, and logs delivered to primary manufacturers that became firewood.

including post, pole, log furniture, and excelsior manufacturers. The following conversion factors were used to convert Scribner board foot volume to cubic feet:

- 5.75 board feet per cubic foot for sawlogs;
- 5.17 board feet per cubic foot for house logs and vigas;
- 1.02 board foot per cubic foot for all other products.

Of the 5,673 MCF of timber received by sawmills, 2,600 MCF (46 percent) was manufactured into finished lumber or other sawn products, and about 114 MCF

USDA Forest Service Resour. Bull. RMRS-RB-13. 2012

39

New Mexico Timber Harvest and Flow, 2007

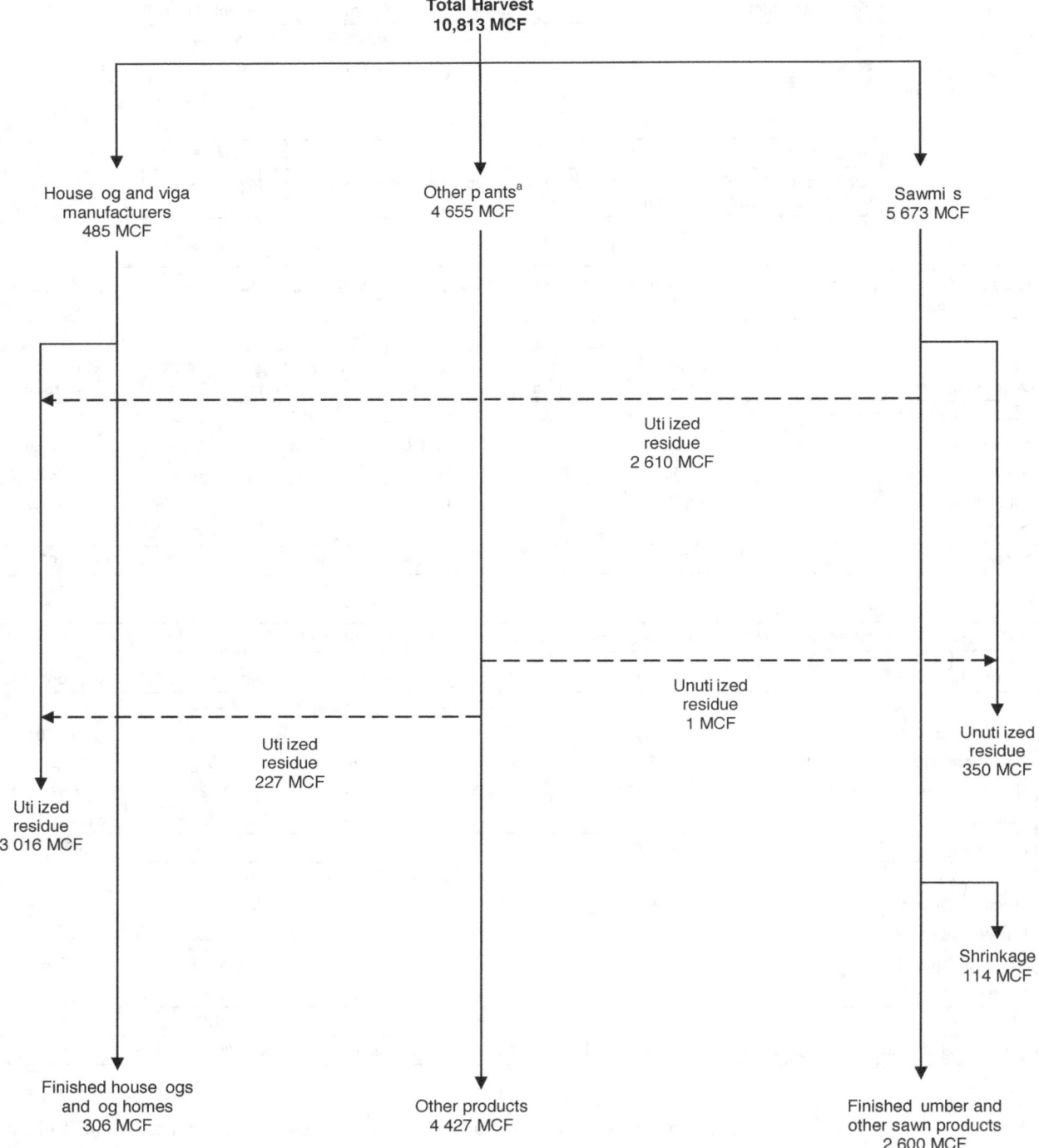

Figure N1: New Mexico timber harvest and flow, 2007.

was lost to shrinkage. The remaining 2,959 MCF (52 percent) yielded mill residue. About 2,610 MCF of sawmill residue was utilized, and about 350 MCF (12 percent) remained unused. Of the 485 MCF of timber received by log home and viga manufacturers, about 306 MCF (63 percent) was used for house logs, while the remaining 179 MCF became mill residue. All of the 179 MCF of house log residue was utilized. Of the 4,655 MCF of timber received by other manufacturers, about 4,427 MCF was utilized in solid wood products such as posts, poles, fuel wood, log furniture, or was used in the production of excelsior. About 227 MCF of residues from these other sectors were utilized, and 1 MCF went unused.

Forest Industry Sectors

New Mexico's primary forest products industry in 2007 consisted of 24 active manufacturers in 12 counties (table N10). Facilities tended to be located near the forest resource in north-central New Mexico and in Otero County (fig. N2). The sawmill sector, manufacturing lumber and other sawn products, was the largest sector operating during 2007, with 12 facilities—9 less mills than were operating in 2002. Five facilities produced vigas and latillas, a decrease of three since 2002. The number of other products manufacturers operating in 2007 remained at seven, with one post and pole manufacturer, one log home producer, two bark product facilities, one firewood producer and two wood shaving/excelsior facilities. Keegan and others (2001b) noted that two particleboard plants and a medium density fiberboard (MDF) facility operated in New Mexico in 1986. One particleboard plant closed in the early 1990s, the MDF plant closed in 1996, and the particleboard facility operating in 1997 was deemed inoperable in 2002 and was thus not included in the current analysis.

Primary wood products sales as well as the number of producers continued to decrease, with finished product sales in 2007 falling 51 percent since 2002 (table N11). The overall drop in sales was due to the dramatic decrease in sawmilling

Table N10: Active New Mexico primary wood products facilities by county and product, 2007 (sources: McLain 1989; Keegan and others 2001b; Morgan and others 2006).

County	Lumber	Vigas and latillas	Other[a]	Total
Bernalillo			1	1
Catron	1			1
Colfax	1		2	3
Grant		1	1	2
Lincoln			1	1
Mora	1			1
Otero	2		2	4
Rio Arriba	1			1
San Miguel	2	1		3
Sandoval	1	1		2
Santa Fe	2	1		3
Taos	1	1		2
2007 Total	**12**	**5**	**7**	**24**
2002 Total	21	8	7	36
1997 Total	22	15	7	44
1986 Total	26	5-10	10	41-46

[a]Other products include posts, poles, log homes, firewood, and bark products.

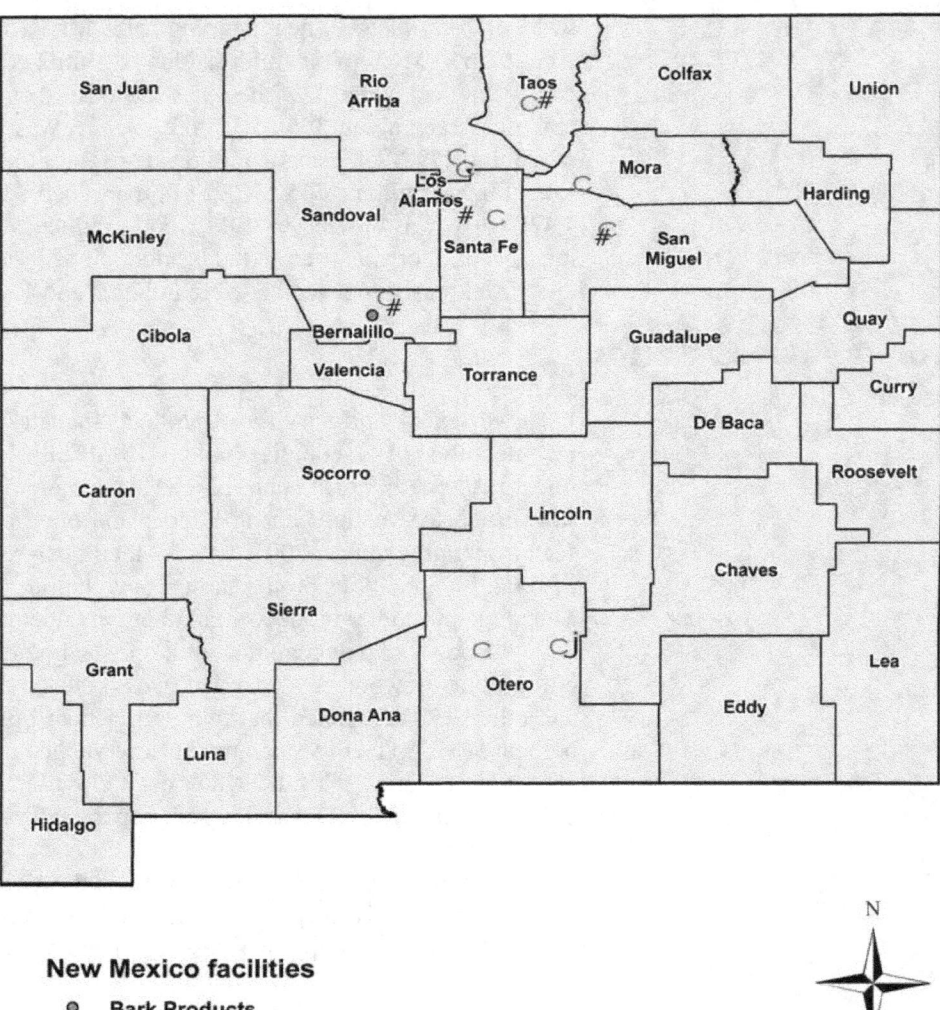

Figure N2: Map of New Mexico facilities.

New Mexico facilities

- ⊙ Bark Products
- j House Log/ Log Home
- C Sawmill
- # Vigas/ Latillas

sales but also in the viga and latilla sectors. Among other products, sales increased 15 percent since 2002. In 1997 and in 2002, lumber accounted for 74 percent of total wood product sales but in 2007 it was only 49 percent. In 2007, sales from other product manufacturers accounted for 39 percent of finished products sales versus nearly 17 percent of sales in 2002.

Sawmill Sector

With the net loss of nine sawmills since 2002, total lumber production in New Mexico dropped 51 percent from about 81.5 MMBF in 2002 to less than 40 MMBF in 2007; most of the State's lumber production shifted to mills producing less than 10 MMBF annually by 2007 (table N12). Closure of those nine mills caused average annual lumber production to fall 15 percent from 3.9 MMBF to 3.3 MMBF per mill (table N13). In 2007, the State's six largest sawmills produced an average of 6.4 MMBF, accounting for 97 percent of lumber production in New Mexico. The remaining 6 mills had an average annual lumber production of less than 204 MBF

Table N11: Finished product sales of New Mexico's primary wood products, selected years (sources: McLain 1989; Miller Freeman, Inc. 1998; Keegan and others 2001b; Morgan and others 2006).

Product	1986	1997	2002	2007
	----Thousand 2007 dollars----			
Lumber and sawn products	$114,881	$53,122	$38,941	$12,616
Vigas and latillas	4,453	12,555	5,225	3,149
Other products[a]	5,566	5,744	8,804	10,102
Total[b]	$124,900	$71,421	$52,970	$25,867

[a]Other products include posts, poles, log homes, log furniture, and bark products.

[b]All sales are reported f.o.b. the manufacturer's plant.

Table N12: New Mexico sawmills by production size class, selected years (sources: Setzer and Wilson 1970; McLain 1989; Keegan and others 2001b; Morgan and others 2006).

Year	Under 10 MMBF[a]	Over 10 MMBF[a]	Total
	-----Number of sawmills-----		
2007	12	c	12
2002	18	3	21
1997	18	4	22
1986	17	9	26
1966	58	6	64
1962	85	c	85
1960	117	c	117
	---Percentage of lumber output---		Volume (MBF[b])
2007	c	c	39,823
2002	12	88	81,515
1997	10	90	108,675
1986	12	88	232,000
1966	38	62	262,848
1962	c	c	242,500
1960	c	c	224,400

[a]Size class is based on reported lumber production. MMBF denotes million board feet lumber tally.

[b]MBF = thousand board feet lumber tally.

[c]In 1960, 1962 and 2007 all mills were included in <10 MMBF to avoid disclosing individual operations.

per mill (table N14). The continued declines in New Mexico's sawmill sector were a direct result of decreasing timber harvests in the State; however, the implementation of restoration and hazardous fuel reduction treatments in the State could spur a recovery of the sawmill sector (Fiedler and others 2002).

On average, New Mexico sawmills produced approximately 1.28 board feet of lumber for every board foot Scribner of timber processed in 2007. Overrun averaged 26 percent in 2002 (Morgan and others 2006). The slight overrun increase from 2002 to 2007 was likely due to the increased proportion of lumber production by larger mills, which typically are more efficient and use smaller logs, and saw a larger proportion of dimension and stud wood. In 2007, lumber produced by New Mexico's sawmills consisted of: 63 percent dimension and studs, 35 percent timbers, and 2 percent board and shop lumber and cants. Dimension lumber accounted for $6.3 million (50 percent) of sawmill product sales in 2007, timbers were about

USDA Forest Service Resour. Bull. RMRS-RB-13. 2012

43

Table N13: Number of New Mexico sawmills and average lumber production, selected years (sources: McLain 1989; Setzer and Wilson 1970; Keegan and others 2001b; Morgan and others 2006).

Year	Number of sawmills	Average production per mill
		MMBF[a]
2007	12	3.3
2002	21	3.9
1997	22	4.9
1986	25	9.2
1966	64	4.1
1962	85	2.9
1960	117	1.9

[a]MMBF = million board feet lumber tally.

Table N14: New Mexico lumber production by mill size, 2007.

Size class[a]	Number of mills	Volume	Percentage of total	Average per mill
		MBF[b]		MBF[b]
Over 1 MMBF	6	38,600	97	6,433
Under 1 MMBF	6	1,223	3	204
Total	12	39,823	100	3,319

[a]Size class is based on reported lumber production. MMBF denotes million board feet lumber tally.

[b]MBF = thousand board feet lumber tally.

$5.9 million (48 percent), and board and shop lumber and cants accounted for $285 thousand (2 percent).

Viga and Latilla Sector

New Mexico's viga and latilla sector continued to contract between 2002 and 2007. Three fewer viga and latilla manufacturers were identified in 2007 than in 2002, and sales dropped by more than $2 million (40 percent). In 2007, the five firms remaining in the sector processed 2,412 MBF Scribner of timber versus 3,393 MBF processed in 2002 (Morgan and others 2006). At just over 828 thousand lineal feet of vigas and latillas produced in 2007, production dropped substantially from 2002 when more than 1 million lineal feet were produced. The continued contraction of the sector in 2007 emphasized the reversal of the previous decade's sector growth noted by Keegan and others (2001b). However, because of the part-time nature of many viga and latilla operations, the sector may again show increased production and sales in the future if demand for traditional styles of construction should increase and if sufficient timber were available.

Other Products Sector

The same mills generally produced other primary wood products in 2007 as in 2002; no new facilities opened during this 5-year period. Product sales by manufacturers of posts, poles, log homes, fire wood, bark and mulch, and wood shavings producers exceeded $10 million in 2007; this was an increase of almost 14 percent over the period. Inflation-adjusted sales from the sector were about $8.8 million in 2002. Additional detail about the sector is withheld to protect the confidentiality of firm level information.

Capacity and Utilization

New Mexico's annual lumber production capacity was 67,425 MBF in 2007. Sawmills produced 39,823 MBF of lumber and utilized about 59 percent of their production capacity. Across all industry sectors, total timber-processing capacity was 61,941 MBF Scribner. Accounting for changes in log inventories, a total of 36,803 MBF Scribner was processed by New Mexico firms in 2007, with total timber-processing capacity utilization about 59 percent. Sawtimber-processing capacity was 170,000 MBF Scribner in 1997, with 48 percent utilized (Keegan and others 2001b). In 2002, sawtimber-processing capacity fell to 88,162 MBF Scribner, with 65,116 MBF Scribner (74 percent) utilized (Morgan and others 2006). Decreased capacity and capacity utilization in the sawmill sector resulted from the permanent closure of large sawmills, which were operating well below capacity in 2002.

Mill Residue Volumes, Types, and Uses

In 1997, Arizona's lone paper mill and the particleboard plant in New Mexico were the largest consumers of mill residues generated in New Mexico. As previously indicated, the paper mill shifted to using recycled material and the particleboard plant closed, thus affecting residue utilization and other aspects of timber-processing in New Mexico and Arizona. Sawmills, New Mexico's leading timber processors, were the main residue producers in the State. Sawmills had to develop new markets for their residues, utilize more of the residues in-house, or consider cutting production to avoid generating more residue than could be disposed of affordably. The lack of outlets for mill residues also negatively impacted the ability of sawmills to process small-diameter timber (Fiedler and others 2002), which typically creates more residue per unit of lumber produced.

During 2007, New Mexico mills produced 42,896 BDUs (approximately 5,820 MCF) of mill residue with 91.4 percent being utilized (table N15). Both residue production and the proportion utilized decreased from 2002, when New Mexico sawmills generated 9,120 MCF, utilizing 95.7 percent (Morgan and others 2006). New Mexico's drop in residue utilization between 2002 and 2007 signaled a reversal of the long-term trend of increased residue utilization noted by Keegan and others (2001b) and was largely attributable to closure of the particleboard plant and changes at the Arizona paper mill. The decrease in total residue volume generated was due to two factors: a substantially smaller volume of timber being processed and sawmills creating fewer residues per unit of lumber produced. In 1997, sawmills produced about 1.22 BDUs per MBF of lumber; by 2007 that residue factor had dropped to 1.03 BDUs per MBF of lumber (table N16).

Coarse residue (chips) was the State's largest residue component at 54.5 percent (23,367 BDU) of all residues in 2007, with 100 percent utilized. Energy facilities used about 22,369 BDUs of the coarse material, with the remaining utilized volume going to unspecified uses (table N15). Fine residues—sawdust and planer shavings—comprised the second largest component at 23.4 percent (10,032 BDU)

Table N15: Production and disposition of New Mexico mill residues, 2007.

Residue type	Total utilized	Pulp and board	Energy	Mulch/ bedding	Unspecified use	Unused	Total produced
			-------Bone-dry units[a]-------				
Coarse	23,359	-	22,369	-	990	8	23,367
Fine	6,562	-	-	6,562	-	3,470	10,032
Sawdust	*3,862*	-	-	*3,862*	-	*3,470*	*7,332*
Planer shavings	*2,700*	-	-	*2,700*	-	-	*2,700*
Bark	9,294	-	291	9,003	-	203	9,497
Total	39,215	-	22,660	15,565	990	3,681	42,896
			-------Percentage of residue type-------				
Coarse	100.0	-	95.7	-	4.2	0.0	54.5
Fine	65.4	-	-	65.4	-	34.6	23.4
Sawdust	*52.7*	-	-	*52.7*	-	*47.3*	*17.1*
Planer shavings	*100.0*	-	-	*100.0*	-	-	*6.3*
Bark	97.9	-	3.1	94.8	-	2.1	22.1
Total	91.4	-	52.8	36.3	2.3	8.6	100.0

[a]Bone-dry unit = 2,400 b oven-dry wood.

Table N16: New Mexico sawmill residue factors, 1997, 2002 and 2007 (source: Keegan and others 2001b; Morgan and others 2006).

Type of residue	1997	2002	2007
	------BDU/MBF lumber tally[a]--------		
Coarse	0.52	0.56	0.58
Sawdust	0.29	0.20	0.17
Planer shavings	0.18	0.15	0.06
Bark	0.23	0.21	0.22
Total	1.22	1.12	1.03

[a]Bone-dry unit (BDU = 2,400 lb oven-dry wood) of residue generated for every 1,000 board feet of lumber manufactured.

of mill residues. Only 65.4 percent of fine residue was utilized in 2007, primarily as mulch and animal bedding. Bark accounted for 22.1 percent of all residues and was largely used for mulch, with 9,294 BDUs (98.0 percent) utilized in 2007.

Primary Forest Products Markets and Sales

Sales from New Mexico's primary wood products industry in 2007 totaled slightly over $26 million, including finished products and mill residues (table N17). Lumber, mine timbers, and other sawn products accounted for 48 percent ($12.6 million) of total sales; other products and mill residues accounted for 40 percent ($10.3 million); while vigas and latillas accounted for 12 percent ($3.1 million). New Mexico was the leading market area for vigas, latillas, and other products, accounting for 86.8 percent of viga and latilla sales and 40.7 percent of other products sales. The other Four Corners States (Arizona, Colorado, and Utah) as well as New Mexico accounted for 46 percent of lumber sales, and other areas (outside the United States) mostly Mexico accounted for more than 35 percent.

Table N17: Destination and sales value of New Mexico's primary wood products and mill residues, 2007.

Product	New Mexico	Other 4-Corner States	Other Rocky Mtn States[a]	Far West[b]	North -east[c]	South[d]	North Central[e]	Other[f]	Total
	--Thousand 2007 dollars--								
Lumber, mine timbers and other sawn products	$4,035	$1,804	$1,080	$1,080	-	$161	-	$4,456	$12,616
Vigas and latillas	2,733	316	-	-	-	100	-	-	3,149
Other products[g]	4,207	3,136	1,210	1,288	-	415	81	-	10,337
Total	$10,975	$5,256	$2,290	$2,368	-	$676	$81	$4,456	$26,102
	--Percentage of product sales by region--								
Lumber, mine timbers and other sawn products	32.0	14.3	8.6	8.6	-	1.3	-	35.3	48.3
Vigas and latillas	86.8	10.0	-	-	-	3.2	-	-	12.1
Other products[g]	40.7	30.3	11.7	12.5	-	4.0	0.8	-	39.6
Total	42.0	20.1	8.8	9.1	-	2.6	0.3	17.1	100.0

[a]Other Rocky Mountains includes Idaho, Montana, Nevada.

[b]Far West includes Alaska, California, Hawaii, Oregon, and Washington.

[c]Northeast includes Connecticut, Maine, Massachusetts, New Hampshire, New Jersey, New York, Pennsylvania, Rhode Island, and Vermont.

[d]South includes Alabama, Arkansas, Delaware, Florida, Georgia, Kentucky, Louisiana, Maryland, Mississippi, North Carolina, Oklahoma, South Carolina, Tennessee, Texas, Virginia, and West Virginia.

[e]North Central includes Illinois, Indiana, Iowa, Kansas, Michigan, Minnesota, Missouri, Nebraska, North Dakota, Ohio, South Dakota, and Wisconsin.

[f]Other areas consist of products being shipped outside the United States.

[g]Other products include posts, poles,log homes, log furniture, bark products, firewood, and mill residues.

Utah

This chapter focuses on Utah's timber harvest and forest products industry during 2007. Details of timber harvest, flow, and use are followed by descriptions of the primary processing sectors, capacity and utilization statistics, and mill residue characteristics. The chapter concludes with information on primary wood products industry sales by Utah mills. Comparisons to previous years are provided where possible. Limited historical information is available about timber harvesting and mill production and residues in Utah. The last comprehensive study of the State's industrial roundwood production and mill residues was conducted in 2002 (Morgan and others 2006), and data for previous years include 1966 (Setzer and Wilson 1970), 1969 (Setzer 1971d), 1970 (Green and Setzer 1974), 1974 (Setzer and Throssell 1977b), and 1992 (Keegan and others 1995).

Timber Harvest, Flow, and Use

In 2008, Utah had approximately 4.1 million acres of nonreserved timberland (U.S. Department of Agriculture, FIDO 2009) with National Forests accounting for 73 percent, private and tribal owners accounting for 18 percent, and other public agencies accounting for the remaining 9 percent (table U1). All private timberland was classified as NIPF timberland. Utah had no large tracts of timberland owned by entities operating primary wood processing facilities. Sawtimber volume on nonreserved timberlands was estimated at 4.8 billion cubic feet or approximately

USDA Forest Service Resour. Bull. RMRS-RB-13. 2012

47

Table U1: Utah nonreserved timberland by ownership class (source: Forest Inventory and Analysis program, 2008).

Ownership class	Thousand acres	Percentage of nonreserved timberland
National Forest	2,982	73
Private and tribal	727	18
Other public	387	9
Total	4,096	100

Table U2: Utah timber products harvested by ownership class, 2007.

Ownership class	Sawlogs	House logs	Other products[a]	All products
	--------------Thousand board feet, Scribner------------------			
National Forests	8,666	5,660	1,164	15,490
Private and tribal timberland	8,679	1,690	1,301	11,669
Other public[b]	330	-	2,832	3,162
All owners	17,675	7,350	5,296	30,321
	----Percentage of harvested product by ownership---			
National Forests	49.0	77.0	22.0	51.1
Private and tribal timberland	49.1	23.0	24.6	38.5
Other public[b]	1.9	-	53.5	10.4
All owners	58.3	24.2	17.5	100

[a]Other products include industrial fuelwood, furniture logs, fiber logs, posts, and poles.

[b]Other ownership class includes BLM and State.

24.8 billion board feet Scribner in 2008 (U.S. Department of Agriculture, FIDO 2009).

Timber Harvest

Utah's 2007 commercial timber harvest was 30.3 MMBF Scribner (table U2), 27 percent less than the 2002 harvest of approximately 41 MMBF Scribner (Morgan and others 2006), and 51 percent less than the 1974 harvest of 62 MMBF (Setzer and Throssell 1977b). The decrease in Utah's total annual timber harvest since 1992 was largely due to the decline in National Forest timber harvest. In 1966 and 1970, National Forests accounted for 94 and 88 percent, respectively, of harvested volume (Setzer and Wilson 1970; Green and Setzer 1974). In 1992, National Forest timber accounted for almost 50.0 MMBF (77 percent) of the annual harvest (Keegan and others 1995); in 2007 the agency provided only 15.5 MMBF (51 percent). As in most of the Western States, decreasing Federal timber harvests have led to greater shares of annual timber harvest coming from other ownership sources. National Forests still provide the majority of the State's harvest, but the volume and proportionate share supplied by private and tribal owners continues to increase. During 2007, private and tribal landowners accounted for 38.5 percent (11.7 MMBF) of Utah's timber harvest, about the same percent as in 2002. National Forests provided the majority (77 percent) of house logs harvested in 2007, but among sawlogs and other products (e.g., furniture logs, fiber logs, posts, poles, and industrial fuelwood) private timberlands and National Forests were evenly split—each providing slightly less than 50 percent (table U2). Sawlogs accounted

Table U3: Utah timber harvest by county, selected years (sources: Setzer and Throssell 1977b; Keegan and others 1995; Morgan and others 2006).

County	1974	1992	2002	2007	1974	1992	2002	2007
	--------MBF Scribner---------				---------Percentage---------			
Beaver	155	2,952	633	468	0.2	4.6	1.5	1.5
Cache	1,389	175	1,180	1,150	2.2	0.3	2.9	3.8
Carbon	260	100	1,670	1,564	0.4	0.2	4.0	5.2
Daggett	3,193	2,850	375	-	5.1	4.4	0.9	-
Davis	-	-	135	-	-	-	0.3	-
Duchesne	2,539	1,767	3,469	1,793	4.1	2.7	8.4	5.9
Emery	250	-	45	284	0.4	-	0.1	0.9
Garfield	8,502	7,047	3,446	3,141	13.6	10.9	8.4	10.4
Grand	5,000	-	20	1,925	8.0	-	a	6.3
Iron	-	1,435	773	1,554	-	2.2	1.9	5.1
Juab	-	-	1	-	-	-	0.0	-
Kane	6,480	4,117	5,520	60	10.4	6.4	13.4	0.2
Millard	30	-	342	-	a	-	0.8	-
Morgan	11	25	250	150	a	a	0.6	0.5
Piute	440	620	3,288	500	0.7	1.0	8.0	1.6
Rich	2,159	-	3,000	-	3.5	-	7.3	-
Salt Lake	-	-	65	59	-	-	0.2	0.2
San Juan	5,000	4,503	1,444	1,865	8.0	7.0	3.5	6.2
Sanpete	520	3,750	2,468	3,800	0.8	5.8	6.0	12.5
Sevier	715	3,663	1,703	1,483	1.1	5.7	4.1	4.9
Summit	5,589	10,000	4,107	2,700	8.9	15.5	10.0	8.9
Uintah	14,652	16,624	2,715	1,398	23.5	25.7	6.6	4.6
Utah	20	-	323	793	a	-	0.8	2.6
Wasatch	1,606	2,908	3,750	4,300	2.6	4.5	9.1	14.2
Washington	-	-	375	1,334	-	-	0.9	4.4
Wayne	3,905	2,110	110	-	6.3	3.3	0.3	-
Weber	50	20	60	-	0.1	a	0.1	-
Total	62,465	64,666	41,268	30,321	100	100	100	100

aLess than 0.05 percent.

for about 58 percent (17.6 MMBF) of the total volume harvested in 2007, house logs were 24 percent, and other products accounted for about 18 percent.

In 2007, Wasatch County led Utah's timber harvest, with 14 percent (4.3 MMBF Scribner) of total volume; Sanpete and Garfield Counties followed with 13 and 10 percent, respectively (table U3). In 2002, Kane and Summit Counties led the harvest with 5.5 MMBF (13 percent) and 4.1 MMBF (10 percent) of the harvest, respectively (Morgan and others 2006).

Spruces, including Engelmann and blue spruce, were the leading species harvested in Utah, accounting for 42 percent (12.6 MMBF) of the harvest in 2007 (table U4). Aspen and cottonwood accounted for 29 percent, lodgepole pine for 13 percent, Douglas-fir accounted for 11 percent while ponderosa pine only accounted for 3 percent of harvest. In 2002, spruce was the leading species harvested, accounting for 44 percent, while lodgepole accounted for 23 percent (Morgan and others 2006). During the 1960s and 1970s, ponderosa pine was the leading species harvested, accounting for 30 to 50 percent of the harvest; while lodgepole pine

USDA Forest Service Resour. Bull. RMRS-RB-13. 2012

49

Table U4: Proportion of Utah timber harvest by species, selected years (sources: Setzer and Wilson 1970; Setzer 1971d; Setzer and Throssell 1977b; Keegan and others 1995; Morgan and others 2006).

Species	1966	1969	1974	1992	2002	2007
	\multicolumn{6}{c}{----------------Percentage of harvest----------------}					
Engelmann spruce	19	13	22	35	44	42
Aspen and cottonwood	c	c	4	5	10	29
Lodgepole pine	18	18	27	46	23	13
Douglas-fir	3	11	8	4	8	11
Ponderosa pine	50	43	33	5	13	3
True firs[a]	4	7	3	5	2	2
Other species[b]	6	8	3	c	c	c
All species	100	100	100	100	100	100

[a]True firs include white, subalpine, and corkbark fir.

[b]Other species include juniper and hardwoods.

[c]Less than 0.5 percent.

Table U5: Utah timber harvest by species and product, 2007.

Species	Sawlogs	House logs	Other products[c]	All products
	\multicolumn{4}{c}{---------------Thousand board feet, Scribner------------}			
Engelmann spruce	6,517	5,635	455	12,607
Aspen and cottonwood	5,122	6	3,601	8,730
Lodgepole pine	1,430	1,372	1,187	3,989
Douglas-fir	2,953	276	31	3,260
Ponderosa pine	1,016	55	10	1,080
True firs[a]	631	6	11	648
Other species[b]	5	0	1	6
All species	17,675	7,350	5,297	30,321
	\multicolumn{4}{c}{------------Percentage of product by species------------}			
Engelmann spruce	36.9	76.7	8.6	41.6
Aspen and cottonwood	29.0	0.1	68.0	28.8
Lodgepole pine	8.1	18.7	22.4	13.2
Douglas-fir	16.7	3.8	0.6	10.8
Ponderosa pine	5.7	0.7	0.2	3.6
True firs[a]	3.6	0.1	0.2	2.1
Other species[b]	d	-	d	d
All species	58.3	24.2	17.5	100

[a]True firs include white, subalpine, and corkbark fir.

[b]Other species include juniper and hardwoods.

[c]Other products include industrial fuelwood, furniture logs, fiber logs, posts, and poles.

[d]Less than 0.1 percent

and spruces each accounted for 15 to 25 percent (Setzer and Wilson 1970; Setzer 1971d; Green and Setzer 1974; Setzer and Throssell 1977b).

Spruces were the leading species harvested for sawlogs and houselogs in 2007, accounting for 6.5 and 5.6 MMBF (37 and 77 percent), respectively (table U5). Aspen and cottonwood accounted for slightly more than 3.6 MMBF (68 percent) of the volume harvested for other products. Lodgepole pine was the leading component of house logs (19 percent) and of other products (22 percent).

Timber Flow

The majority (83 percent) of Utah's 2007 timber harvest was processed in-State; however, Utah was a net exporter of almost 2.9 MMBF of timber. About 5.2 MMBF were exported for processing in Colorado, Wyoming, Idaho, and Arizona; while 2.3 MMBF were imported for processing in Utah from Arizona, Colorado, Idaho, Montana, Wyoming, and as far away as Oregon and Canada (table U6).

Timber processors in Utah received 27,470 MBF of timber in 2007, including 2,336 MBF that was harvested outside the State. Private and tribal timberlands provided 11,587 MBF (42 percent) of the timber delivered to Utah mills in 2007 (table U7). National Forests provided 56 percent (15,502 MBF) of timber receipts, with more than half (14) of Utah's timber processors receiving timber cut from National Forests. In 2002, Utah mills received 18 percent more timber. National Forests supplied 67 percent (21,898 MBF) of the timber in 2002, and private and tribal owners supplied 28 percent (9,241 MBF). During 2007, National Forests provided Utah timber processors with 68 percent of house logs, 54 percent of sawlogs, and 52 percent of other timber products including fiber logs, furniture logs, and posts, and poles (table U8). NIPF and tribal landowners provided 45 percent of sawlogs, 32 percent of houselogs, and 46 percent of other timber products. State lands provided less than 1 percent of the timber received by mills in Utah.

Timber Use

Utah's 2007 timber harvest—approximately 7,082 MCF, exclusive of bark (fig. U1)—was used by several manufacturing sectors both within and outside of Utah. Of this volume, 3,459 MCF went as logs to sawmills, 1,842 MCF went to log home manufacturers, and 1,781 MCF went to other plants, including post, pole,

Table U6: Utah timber products imports and exports, 2007.

Timber product	Imports	Exports	Net imports (net exports)
	---Thousand board feet, Scribner---		
Sawlogs	1,433	200	1,233
House logs	432	1,275	(843)
Other products[a]	471	3,712	(3,241)
All products	2,336	5,187	(2,851)

[a]Other products include industrial fuelwood, furniture logs, fiber logs, posts, and poles.

Table U7: Ownership of timber products received by Utah mills, 1992, 2002 and 2007 (sources: Keegan and others 1995; Morgan and others 2006).

	1992		2002		2007	
Ownership class	MBF Scribner	Percentage of total	MBF Scribner	Percentage of total	MBF Scribner	Percentage of total
Private and tribal timberland	11,341	19.3	9,241	28.4	11,587	42.2
Public timberland	46,927	79.9	23,245	71.5	15,732	57.3
National Forest	*46,595*	*79.3*	*21,898*	*67.3*	*15,502*	*56.4*
State lands	*332*	*0.6*	*1,346*	*4.1*	*230*	*0.8*
Other owners[a]	485	0.8	33	0.1	152	0.6
All owners	58,753	100	32,518	100	27,470	100

[a]Other owners include the BLM, Canada, and (for 1992) unknown owners.

USDA Forest Service Resour. Bull. RMRS-RB-13. 2012

51

Table U8: Timber received by Utah forest products industry by ownership class and product, 2007.

Ownership class	Sawlogs	House logs	Other products[b]	All products
	---------------Thousand board feet, Scribner------------			
Private and tribal timberland	8,579	2,062	946	11,587
Public timberland	10,229	4,444	1,058	15,731
National forest	*9,999*	*4,444*	*1,058*	*15,501*
State lands	*230*	-	-	*230*
Other owners[a]	100	-	52	152
All owners	18,908	6,506	2,056	27,470
	------------Percentage of product by owner-------------			
Private and tribal timberland	45.4	31.7	46.0	42.2
Public timberland	54.1	68.3	51.5	57.3
National forest	*52.9*	*68.3*	*51.5*	*56.4*
State lands	*1.2*	-	-	*0.8*
Other owners[a]	0.5	-	2.5	0.6
All owners	68.8	23.7	7.5	100

[a]Other owners include the BLM and Canada.

[b]Other products include furniture logs, fiber logs, posts, and poles.

log furniture, and excelsior manufacturers. The following conversion factors were used to convert Scribner board foot volume to cubic feet:

- 4.81 board feet per cubic foot for house logs;
- 5.15 board feet per cubic foot for sawlogs;
- 2.05 board foot per cubic foot for all other products.

Of the 3,459 MCF of timber received by sawmills, 1,640 MCF (47 percent) was milled into finished lumber or other sawn products, and about 69 MCF was lost to shrinkage. The remaining 1,750 MCF (51 percent) yielded mill residue. About 1,715 MCF of sawmill residue was utilized, and about 35 MCF (2 percent) remained unused. Of the 1,842 MCF of timber received by log home manufacturers, about 1,106 MCF (60 percent) was processed into house logs, while the remaining 736 MCF became mill residue. About 684 MCF of house log residue was utilized, and about 52 MCF remained unused. Of the 1,781 MCF of timber received by other manufacturers, about 1,773 MCF was utilized as solid wood products such as posts, poles and log furniture. About 7 MCF of residues from these other sectors were utilized, and 1 MCF went unused.

Forest Industry Sectors

Utah's primary forest products industry in 2007 consisted of 27 active manufacturers in 13 counties (table U9). Facilities tended to be located near the forest resource along the mountainous central spine of the State (fig. U2). Changes in Utah's industry structure over the past 25 years were similar to those experienced throughout the West, with the number of sawmills decreasing and the number and diversity of other manufacturers increasing (Keegan and others 1995, 2001 a,b; Morgan and others 2004 a,b; Morgan and others 2006). The sawmill sector (manufacturing lumber and other sawn products) was the largest, and included 12 mills in 2007; 10 facilities produced house logs and log homes and there were five log

Utah Timber Harvest and Flow, 2007

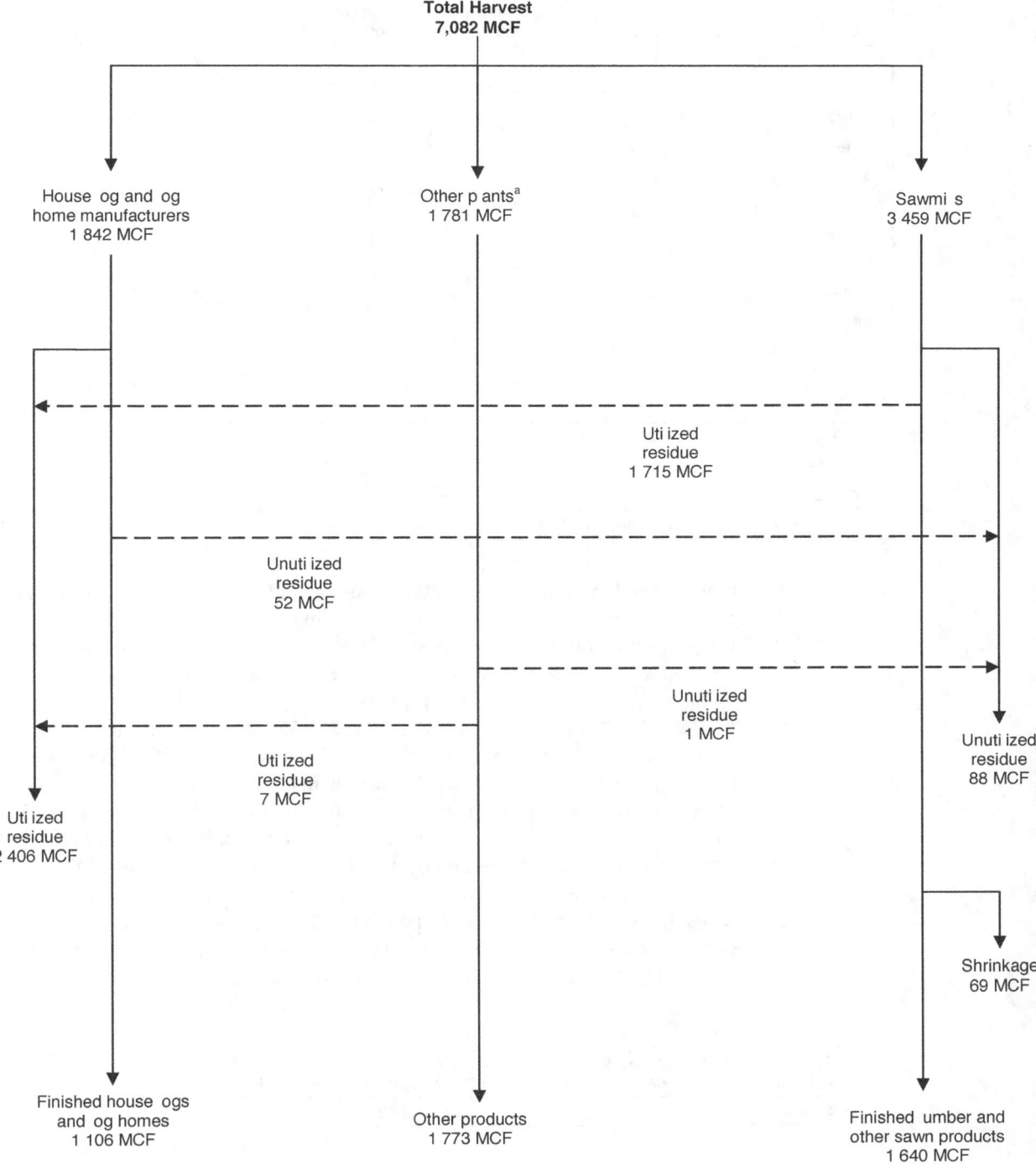

Total Harvest
7,082 MCF

House og and og
home manufacturers
1 842 MCF

Other p ants[a]
1 781 MCF

Sawmi s
3 459 MCF

Uti ized
residue
1 715 MCF

Unuti ized
residue
52 MCF

Unuti ized
residue
1 MCF

Unuti ized
residue
88 MCF

Uti ized
residue
7 MCF

Uti ized
residue
2 406 MCF

Shrinkage
69 MCF

Finished house ogs
and og homes
1 106 MCF

Other products
1 773 MCF

Finished umber and
other sawn products
1 640 MCF

Figure U1: Utah timber harvest and flow, 2007

USDA Forest Service Resour. Bull. RMRS-RB-13. 2012

53

Table U9: Active Utah primary wood products facilities by county and product, 2007 (sources: Keegan and others 1995; Morgan and others 2006).

County	Lumber	Log homes and house logs	Log furniture and other products[a]	Total
Beaver	1		1	2
Cache	2		1	3
Duchesne	2	1		3
Garfield	1			1
Iron	1			1
Morgan	1			1
Salt Lake	1		2	3
Sanpete		1		1
Summit	3			3
Uintah		5		5
Utah			1	1
Wasatch		2		2
Weber		1		1
2007 Total	**12**	**10**	**5**	**27**
2002 Total	23	14	12	49
1992 Total	34	13	4	51

[a]Other products include posts, poles, and bark products.

furniture producers operating in 2007. Morgan and others (2006) identified 49 primary wood-processing plants in 2002, including 23 sawmills, 14 house log plants, 10 log furniture producers, one post and pole firm, and a decorative bark producer. In 1966 there were 50 active sawmills in the State (Setzer and Wilson 1970).

The number of producers, and primary wood products sales decreased between 2002 and 2007. Finished product sales ($27,332,000—adjusted for inflation) in 2007 were about 30 percent lower than 2002 sales, (table U10). This overall decrease was coupled with a substantial decline in lumber and log home sales while a slight increase was noted in other product sales. Lumber sales were down $6.5 million, and log home manufacturers sales decreased around $6 million; however the sales of other products increased by about $875 thousand over the 2002 totals. In 2007, lumber sales accounted for less than 30 percent of finished product sales, versus 40 percent in 2002 and 73 percent in 1992; house logs and log homes accounted for about the same in 2002 and 2007 (55 percent) of sales. Other product sales nearly doubled to 15 percent in 2007 compared to 8 percent of total sales in 2002.

Table U10: Finished product sales of Utah's primary wood products sectors, 1992, 2002 and 2007 (sources: Keegan and others 1995; Morgan and others 2006).

Sector	1992	2002	2007
	---Thousands of 2007 dollars---[b]		
Sawmills	$27,389	$14,628	$8,114
Log homes	9,208	21,007	15,053
Other sectors[a]	982	3,290	4,165
Total[b]	$37,579	$38,925	$27,332

[a]Other sectors include producers of posts, poles, and log furniture. Mill residues, firewood, mulch, and bark products not included for comparison to previous years.

[b]All sales are reported f.o.b. the manufacturer's plant.

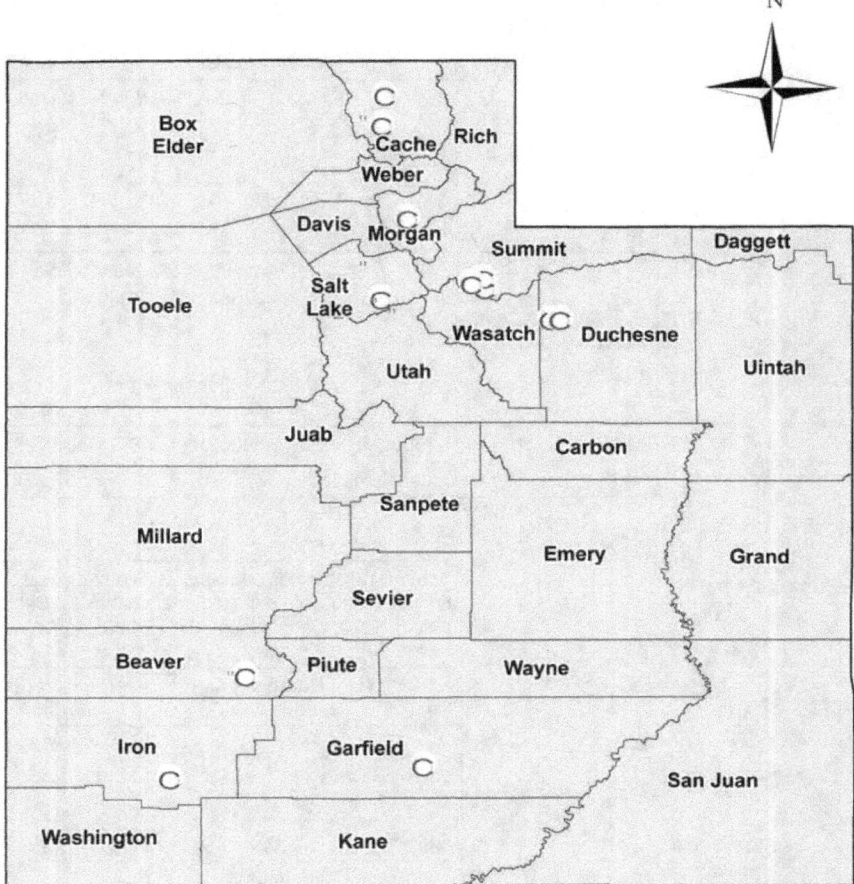

Figure U2: Map of Utah
facilities.

Utah facilities

j   **House Log/Log Home**

"   **Log Furniture**

C   **Sawmill**

Sawmill Sector

Utah's sawmill sector has been in decline for several decades. Lumber production in 2007 was 14 percent lower than in 2002, 64 percent lower than in 1992 and 68 percent lower than in 1966, while the number of mills declined 48, 32, and 54 percent over the same periods (table U11). Most of the production loss was among the State's larger mills that produced more than 1 MMBF of lumber annually, while the greatest loss of milling facilities was among the small mills. The proportion of lumber production by large versus small mills has increased with larger mills contributing 94 percent of the production, but the average annual lumber production per mill has returned to the 1992 level (table U12). Average annual lumber production among the State's five largest mills was about 4.3 MMBF lumber tally in 2007 (table U13), compared to 3.8 MMBF among six mills in 2002.The remaining 7 small mills had an average lumber production of 182 MBF

USDA Forest Service Resour. Bull. RMRS-RB-13. 2012

55

Table U11: Utah sawmills by production size class, selected years (sources: Setzer and Wilson 1970; Keegan and others 1995; Morgan and others 2006).

Year	Under 1 MMBF[a]	Over 1 MMBF[a]	Total
	------------------*Number of sawmills*------------------		
2007	7	5	12
2002	17	6	23
1992	25	9	34
1966	37	13	50
	---*Percentage of lumber output*---		*Volume (MBF[b])*
2007	6	94	22,892
2002	13	87	26,524
1992	13	87	63,637
1966	10	90	72,000

[a]Size class is based on reported lumber production. MMBF = million board feet lumber tally.

[b]MBF = thousand board feet lumber tally.

Table U12: Number of Utah sawmills and average lumber production, selected years (sources: Setzer and Wilson 1970; Keegan and others 1995; Morgan and others 2006).

Year	Number of sawmills	Average production per mill
		MMBF[a]
2007	12	1.9
2002	23	1.2
1992	34	1.9
1966	50	1.4

[a]MMBF = million board feet lumber tally.

Table U13: Utah lumber production by mill size, 2007.

Size class[a]	Number of mills	Volume	Percentage of total	Average per mill
		MBF[b]		*MBF[b]*
Over 1 MMBF	5	21,621	94	4,324
Under 1 MMBF	7	1,271	6	182
Total	12	22,892	100	1,908

[a]Size class is based on reported lumber production. MMBF denotes million board feet lumber tally.

[b]MBF = thousand board feet lumber tally.

in 2007, compared to the 2002 average production of 204 MBF at 17 small mills (Morgan and others 2006).

On average, Utah sawmills produced approximately 1.20 board feet of lumber for every board foot Scribner of timber processed. This average overrun of 20 percent in 2007 contrasts sharply with the 2002 overrun of 28 percent (Morgan and others 2006). The decrease in overrun over the past 5 years indicates a possible shift in products manufactured, smaller and lower quality logs utilized, or that few sawmills in Utah have invested in improved milling technology.

Sales from sawmills accounted for just 30 percent ($8.1 million) of Utah timber processors' finished products sales in 2007. This proportion of sales from sawmills was the smallest of the Four Corners States. Sales from sawmills accounted for more than 56 percent of sales in Arizona, 49 percent of sales in New Mexico and more than 45 percent in Colorado during 2007. Board and shop lumber accounted for almost $4.5 million (55 percent) of sawmill product sales in 2007; dimension lumber and studs accounted for almost $2.4 million (30 percent), timbers and cants accounted for $1.2 million (14 percent); and other sawn products accounted for the balance (<1 percent) of finished product sales from sawmills.

Log Home Sector

Sales value from Utah's log home sector decreased over the past 5 years. This sector lost facilities during the period with 10 house log manufacturers identified in 2007—four less than in 2002. Only firms that processed timber and manufactured house logs or log homes, not log home distributors, were included in the 1992, 2002, and 2007 censuses. In 2007, Utah's 10 log home manufacturers processed 7.3 MMBF of timber, produced about 6.2 MMLF of house logs, and generated about $15 million in product sales. By sales value, Utah's log home sector is the fourth largest in the Western United States behind Montana, Idaho, and Colorado.

Other Products Sectors

A significant decrease occurred in the number of facilities among Utah's other products sectors, with less than half as many facilities operating in 2007 than in 2002; however, sales of the other products sector was greatly increased from 2002. There were five other product facilities in 2007 that produced log furniture and post and poles. Sales of posts, poles, and log furniture totaled almost $4.2 million in 2007. Additional detail about the sector is withheld to protect the confidentiality of firm level information.

Capacity and Utilization

Utah's annual sawmill lumber production capacity was 46.5 MMBF in 2007. Sawmills produced 22.9 MMBF of lumber and utilized 49 percent of their lumber production capacity. This was the lowest level of sawmill production capacity utilization for all the Four Corners States in 2007. Timber-processing capacity among Utah sawmills was 39,172 MBF Scribner, with 18,945 MBF Scribner of timber processed, making utilization of timber-processing capacity among sawmills about 48 percent in 2007. Such low levels of capacity utilization often signal the closure of mills and this was no exception for Utah, which saw the closure and out-of-State relocation of its second largest sawmill during 2003. Across all industry sectors, total timber-processing capacity was 60,062 MBF Scribner. Accounting for changes in mills' log inventories, a total of 26,371 MBF Scribner was processed by Utah firms in 2007, making timber-processing capacity utilization about 44 percent across all sectors.

Mill Residue Volumes, Types, and Uses

Across all sectors, Utah timber processors produced 27,645 BDU (approximately 2,654 MCF) of mill residue, with 87 percent being utilized (table U14). Total residue production declined slightly from 3,288 MCF in 2002, and the proportion utilized decreased slightly from 89 percent (Morgan and others 2006). Utah's

Table U14: Production and disposition of Utah mill residues, 2007.

Residue type	Total utilized	Pulp and board	Energy	Mulch/ bedding	Unspecified use	Unused	Total produced
			------- Bone-dry units[a] -------				
Coarse	10,534	-	2,050	-	8,484	2,412	12,946
Fine	9,281	-	4	6,833	2,444	223	9,504
Sawdust	*5,306*	*-*	*4*	*3,280*	*2,022*	*148*	*5,454*
Planer shavings	*3,975*	*-*	*-*	*3,553*	*422*	*75*	*4,050*
Bark	4,281	-	4	3,726	551	914	5,195
Total	24,096	-	2,058	10,559	11,479	3,549	27,645
			------- Percentage of residue type -------				
Coarse	81.4	-	15.8	-	65.5	18.6	46.8
Fine	97.7	-	0.0	71.9	25.7	2.3	34.4
Sawdust	*97.3*	*-*	*0.1*	*60.1*	*37.1*	*2.7*	*19.7*
Planer shavings	*98.1*	*-*	*-*	*87.7*	*10.4*	*1.9*	*14.7*
Bark	82.4	-	0.1	71.7	10.6	17.6	18.8
Total	87.2	-	7.4	38.2	41.5	12.8	100

[a]Bone-dry unit = 2,400 b oven-dry wood.

decreased residue production resulted from decreased timber volumes processed, while residue utilization remained constant and was attributable to the evolution of better uses for residue-related products, especially bark and coarse residues. Sawmills, the leading timber processors, were also the main residue producers in Utah, producing 1.0 BDU of residue per MBF of lumber in 2007 (table U15).

Coarse residue was the State's largest residue component at 46.8 percent (12,946 BDU) of all residues in 2007, with 81.4 percent utilized. In-State facilities used 8,484 BDU of the coarse material for unspecified uses, with the remaining utilized volume going to energy. Fine residues—sawdust and planer shavings—comprised the second largest component at 34.4 percent (9,504 BDU) of mill residues. More than 97 percent of fine residue was utilized in 2007, primarily as mulch or animal bedding, with about one-fourth of fine residues going to unspecified uses. Bark accounted for 19 percent of all residues and was largely used for mulch or unspecified uses, with 4,281 BDU (82 percent) utilized.

Table U15: Utah sawmill residue factors, 1992, 2002 and 2007 (source: Keegan and others 1995; Morgan and others 2006).

Type of residue	1992	2002	2007
	------ BDU/MBF lumber tally[a] --------		
Coarse	0.56	0.48	0.44
Sawdust	0.19	0.19	0.21
Planer shavings	0.06	0.10	0.15
Bark	0.28	0.21	0.20
Total	1.09	0.98	1.00

[a]Bone-dry unit (BDU = 2,400 lb oven-dry wood) of residue generated for every 1,000 board feet of lumber manufactured.

Primary Forest Products Markets and Sales

Sales from Utah's primary wood products industry during 2007 totaled nearly $28.6 million, including finished products and mill residues (table U16). House logs and log homes accounted for 56 percent (more than $16 million) of total sales; lumber, mine timbers, and other sawn products accounted for about 33 percent (almost $9.6 million); while other products and mill residues accounted for 10 percent (nearly $3 million). Utah was the leading market area for lumber, log homes, posts, poles, and log furniture, with in-State sales accounting for almost 35 percent of total sales. The other Four Corners States (Arizona, Colorado, and New Mexico) accounted for about 32 percent of total sales, with log homes accounting for 74 percent of sales in the region. The South accounted for 13 percent of total sales, with log homes accounting for 82 percent of sales to the South. Following Utah, the North Central area was a major market area for lumber and other sawn products.

Table U16: Destination and sales value of Utah's primary wood products and mill residues, 2007.

Product	Utah	Other 4-Corner States	Other Rocky Mtn States[a]	Far West[b]	North-east[c]	South[d]	North Central[e]	Other[f]	Total
	--Thousand 2007 dollars--								
Lumber, mine timbers, and other sawn products	$3,803	$2,166	$76	-	$111	$445	$2,959	-	$9,560
House logs and log homes	4,469	6,732	1,000	200	600	3,032	-	40	16,073
Other products[g]	1,614	191	51	51	338	230	486	-	2,961
Total	$9,886	$9,089	$1,127	$251	$1,049	$3,707	$3,445	$40	$28,594
	---------------------------------Percentage of regional sales by product---------------------------------								
Lumber, mine timbers, and other sawn products	38.5	23.8	6.7	-	10.6	12.0	85.9	-	33.4
House logs and log homes	45.2	74.1	88.7	79.7	57.2	81.8	-	100.0	56.2
Other products[g]	16.3	2.1	4.5	20.3	32.2	6.2	14.1	-	10.4
Total	34.6	31.8	3.9	0.9	3.7	13.0	12.0	0.1	100

[a]Other Rocky Mountains includes Idaho, Montana, Nevada.

[b]Far West includes Alaska, California, Hawaii, Oregon, and Washington.

[c]Northeast includes Connecticut, Maine, Massachusetts, New Hampshire, New Jersey, New York, Pennsylvania, Rhode Island, and Vermont.

[d]South includes Alabama, Arkansas, Delaware, Florida, Georgia, Kentucky, Louisiana, Maryland, Mississippi, North Carolina, Oklahoma, South Carolina, Tennessee, Texas, Virginia, and West Virginia.

[e]North Central includes Illinois, Indiana, Iowa, Kansas, Michigan, Minnesota, Missouri, Nebraska, North Dakota, Ohio, South Dakota, and Wisconsin.

[f]Other areas consist of products being shipped outside the United States.

[g]Other products include posts, poles, log furniture, mill residues, firewood, mulch, and bark products.

USDA Forest Service Resour. Bull. RMRS-RB-13. 2012

59

References

Fiedler, C.E., C.E. Keegan, S.H. Robertson, T.A. Morgan, C.W. Woodall, and J. Chmelik. 2002. A strategic assessment of fire hazard in New Mexico. Report submitted to National Joint Fire Sciences Program, Boise, ID. 27 p.

Green, A.W. and T.S. Setzer 1974. The Rocky Mountain timber situation, 1970. Resour. Bull. INT-10. Ogden, UT: U.S. Department of Agriculture, Forest Service, Intermountain Forest and Range Experiment Station. 78 p.

Keegan, C.E., A.L. Chase, T.A. Morgan, S.E. Bodmer, D.D. Van Hooser, and M. Mortimer. 2001a. Arizona's forest products industry: a descriptive analysis 1998. Missoula: The University of Montana, Bureau of Business and Economic Research. 20 p.

Keegan, C.E., A.L. Chase, T.A. Morgan, S.E. Bodmer, D.D. Van Hooser, and M. Mortimer. 2001b. New Mexico's forest products industry: a descriptive analysis 1997. Missoula: The University of Montana, Bureau of Business and Economic Research. 24 p.

Keegan, C.E., K. Gebert, A.L. Chase, T.A. Morgan, S.E. Bodmer, and D.D. Van Hooser. 2001c. Montana's forest products industry: a descriptive analysis 1969-2000. Missoula: The University of Montana, Bureau of Business and Economic Research. 67 p.

Keegan, C.E., D.P. Wichman, and D.D. Van Hooser. 1995. Utah's forest products industry: a descriptive analysis, 1992. Resour. Bull. INT-RB-83. Ogden, UT: U.S. Department of Agriculture, Forest Service, Intermountain Research Station. 21 p.

Lockwood-Post. 2008. 2008 Lockwood-Post's directory of the pulp, paper and allied trades. San Francisco, CA: Lockwood-Post. 515 p.

Lynch, D.L. and K. Mackes. 2001. Wood use in Colorado at the turn of the twenty-first century. Res. Pap. RMRS-RP-32. Fort Collins, CO: U.S. Department of Agriculture, Forest Service, Rocky Mountain Research Station. 23 p.

McLain, W.H. 1985. Colorado's industrial roundwood production and mill residue, 1982. Resour. Bull. INT-35. Ogden, UT: U.S. Department of Agriculture, Forest Service, Intermountain Research Station. 13 p.

McLain, W.H. 1988. Arizona's timber production and mill residue, 1984. Resour. Bull. INT-55. Ogden, UT: U.S. Department of Agriculture, Forest Service, Intermountain Research Station. 16 p.

McLain, W.H. 1989. New Mexico's timber production and mill residue, 1986. Resour. Bull. INT-59. Ogden, UT: U.S. Department of Agriculture, Forest Service, Intermountain Research Station. 17 p.

Morgan, T.A., T. Dillon, C.E. Keegan, A.L. Chase and M.T. Thompson. 2006. The Four Corners timber harvest and forest products industry, 2002. Resour. Bull. RMRS-RB-7. Fort Collins, CO: U.S. Department of Agriculture, Forest Service, Rocky Mountain Research Station. 64 p.

Morgan, T.A., C.E. Keegan, T. Dillon, A.L. Chase, J.S. Fried, and M.N. Weber. 2004a. California's forest products industry: a descriptive analysis. Gen. Tech. Rep. PNW-GTR-615. Portland, OR: U.S. Department of Agriculture, Forest Service, Pacific Northwest Research Station. 54 p.

Morgan, T.A., C.E. Keegan, T.P. Spoelma, T. Dillon, A.L. Hearst, F.G Wagner, and L.T. DeBlander. 2004b. Idaho's forest products industry: a descriptive analysis. Resour. Bull. RMRS-RB-4. Ogden, UT: U.S. Department of Agriculture, Forest Service, Rocky Mountain Research Station. 31 p.

O'Brien, R.A. 2003. New Mexico's forests, 2000. Resour. Bull. RMRS-RB-3. Ogden, UT: U.S. Department of Agriculture, Forest Service, Rocky Mountain Research Station. 117 p.

Quarterly Census of Employment and Wages [QCEW]. 2004. U.S. Department of Labor, Bureau of Labor Statistics. Quarterly census of employment and wages. www.bls.gov/cew/home htm. (October 2004).

Random Lengths. 2008. Big book 2008: the buyers and sellers directory of the forest products industry. Eugene, OR: Random Lengths Publications, Inc. 1024 p.

Regional Economic Information System [REIS]. 2004. U.S.Department of Commerce, Bureau of Economic Analysis. Regional accounts data. www.bea.gov/bea/regioanl/data.htm. (October 2004).

Setzer, T.S. 1971a. Estimates of timber products output and plant residues, Arizona, 1969. Res. Note INT-130. Ogden, UT: U.S. Department of Agriculture, Forest Service, Intermountain Forest and Range Experiment Station. 4 p.

Setzer, T.S. 1971b. Estimates of timber products output and plant residues, Colorado, 1969. Res. Note INT-131.Ogden, UT: U.S. Department of Agriculture, Forest Service, Intermountain Forest and Range Experiment Station. 4 p.

Setzer, T.S. 1971c. Estimates of timber products output and plant residues, New Mexico, 1969. Res. Note INT-134. Ogden, UT: U.S. Department of Agriculture, Forest Service, Intermountain Forest and Range Experiment Station. 4 p.

Setzer, T.S. 1971d. Estimates of timber products output and plant residues, Utah and Nevada, 1969. Res. Note INT-135. Ogden, UT: U.S. Department of Agriculture, Forest Service, Intermountain Forest and Range Experiment Station. 4 p.

Setzer, T.S. and M.K. Barrett. 1977. New Mexico timber production and mill residues, 1974. Res. Note INT-231.Ogden, UT: U.S. Department of Agriculture, Forest Service, Intermountain Forest and Range Experiment Station. 6 p.

Setzer, T.S. and D.G. Shupe. 1977. Colorado timber production and mill residues, 1974. Res. Note INT-232.Ogden, UT: U.S. Department of Agriculture, Forest Service, Intermountain Forest and Range Experiment Station. 6 p.

Setzer, T.S. and T.S.Throssell. 1977a. Arizona timber production and mill residues, 1974. Res. Note INT-230.Ogden, UT: U.S. Department of Agriculture, Forest Service, Intermountain Forest and Range Experiment Station. 6 p.

Setzer, T.S. and T.S.Throssell. 1977b. Utah timber production and mill residues, 1974. Res. Note INT-234. Ogden, UT: U.S. Department of Agriculture, Forest Service, Intermountain Forest and Range Experiment Station. 5 p.

Setzer, T.S. and A.K. Wilson. 1970. Timber products in the Rocky Mountain States, 1966. Resour. Bull. INT-9. Ogden, UT: U.S. Department of Agriculture, Forest Service, Intermountain Forest and Range Experiment Station. 93 p.

Silver v. Thomas 924 F.Supp. 976 (D. Ariz. 1995).

Spencer, J.S. and T.O. Farrenkopf. 1964. Timber products output in Colorado, Wyoming, and western South Dakota, 1962. Res. Pap. INT-14. Ogden, UT: U.S. Department of Agriculture, Forest Service, Intermountain Forest and Range Experiment Station. 18 p.

U.S. Department of Agriculture, Forest Service, 2009. Forest Inventory Data Online (FIDO) [Database]. FIDO version 1.3 1r1. Washington, DC. http://fiatools fs fed.us/fido/index html. (10 April 2010).

Western Wood Products Association [WWPA]. 1965-2008. Statistical yearbook of the Western lumber industry. Portland, OR: Western Wood Products Association.

Wilson, A.K. and J.S. Spencer, Jr. 1967.Timber resources and industries in the Rocky Mountain States. Resour. Bull. INT-7. Ogden, UT: U.S. Department of Agriculture, Forest Service, Intermountain Forest and Range Experiment Station. 67 p.

www.ingramcontent.com/pod-product-compliance
Lightning Source LLC
Chambersburg PA
CBHW08124528052
45787CB00006B/2810